Mind Openers

JOHN O'KEEFFE has achieved extraordinary personal and business success. He became a hockey international at 19 and his own boss at 21. He taught himself Mandarin, has travelled all over the world and at 38 became managing director of a world famous company.

By the same author:

YOUR ONE WEEK WAY TO MIND-FITNESS
YOUR ONE WEEK WAY TO PERSONAL SUCCESS

Mind Openers for Managers

Your One Week Way to Greater Creativity

John O'Keeffe

Regional Vice-President
Procter & Gamble Europe

Thorsons
An Imprint of HarperCollinsPublishers

Thorsons
An Imprint of HarperCollins*Publishers*
77–85 Fulham Palace Road
Hammersmith, London W6 8JB

1160 Battery Street
San Francisco, California 94111–1213

Published by Thorsons 1994

9 7 5 3 1 10 8 6 4 2

© John O'Keeffe 1994

John O'Keeffe asserts the moral right to
be identified as the author of this work

A catalogue record for this book
is available from the British Library

ISBN 0 7225 3009 9

Typeset by Harper Phototypesetters Limited
Northampton, England
Printed in Great Britain by
HarperCollinsManufacturing Glasgow

This book is dedicated to my parents,
Maurice and Anne O'Keeffe, who brought me up
to believe anything is possible, given an
open mind; and to Jeannie, Tim, Sam and Kelly,
who supplied several of the examples to show
how closed my mind still is.

Contents

How to achieve bigger and better things

Much of our lives is spent on trying to achieve bigger and better things. This is true in school, in sports, in pastimes, in work and in organizations.

The way we do this is relatively simple:

• Set new, stretching goals.
• Find better ways to reach them.

We all know that this simple method is the way to do better in life. So why is it so very difficult to put into practice?

The answer is that we lose much of our potential through having a limited mind-set. This means we limit ourselves, both in realizing how much we can achieve and in what we can do to achieve it. We are often not aware of it, but it happens to us as individuals and it happens to groups or organizations.

How *well* can we do?

Consider how often an organization achieves bigger and better things following a change in the leadership or with new people on the job. Are the newcomers really intrinsically that much better or smarter than those they replace? Or is it that they bring a new attitude, a new perspective, a new mind-set? Imagine the power we could release if we could achieve these changes in mind-set and perspective without the need for changing people. To do this we need to be able to adopt new mind-sets, new ideas of what is possible, and to make a fresh start. This is what 'mind openers' can help us do. They can help us realize how *well* we can do.

What *can* be done?

It is easy to get stuck in a fixed and limited way of doing things. Think how often we dismiss alternative suggestions. There is a way to reject a new idea for doing things for every day of the week:

Monday: 'There's nothing in that idea.'
Tuesday: 'Can't see how that can be done.'
Wednesday: 'There's only one way to look at it.'
Thursday: 'Judgement based on the facts says it won't work.'
Friday: 'It won't work; if you do that, this happens.'
Saturday: 'It won't work when it comes to the details.'
Sunday: 'It's just impossible.'

By the end of the week any new way to bigger and better things is dead!

By 'setting' our minds on a particular approach, we limit our potential. Removing this fixed way of looking at things is the role of mind openers. They show what *can* be done.

Why do minds become 'set' and need opening?

A mind-set is the way you set your mind to look at things. It is easy to develop a limited mind-set based on a few facts and a bias or prejudice. And once your mind is made up, your brain can supply all sorts of reasons to justify your position. It is capable of selecting only those facts that support the mind-set you've taken. It is capable of remembering only those facts that support the position you've taken. Your mind becomes 'closed' and needs to be opened.

As an illustration of this, consider how often the following sorts of phrases are used:

'They have a closed mind on this.'
'He has a mental block when it comes to that.'
'She just can't see it.'
'They have a blind spot on this.'
'He has a short-sighted view.'
'It hasn't dawned on her yet.'
'They are turning a deaf ear.'
'He is just narrow-minded on the subject.'
'She can't see the light of day.'
'They look at it in such a limited way.'
'His mind is stubborn on it.'
'She is fixed in her attitude.'
'Their bias is unshakeable.'
'His mind is made up and we can't change it.'

Some of your mind-sets may be quite deeply ingrained. Descriptions of them can range from a 'judgement' to a 'strongly held opinion' to a 'bias' to a 'prejudice'—but you may take them as 'truths'. Most mind-sets, however, are simply conclusions you have drawn. They are not the *only way* you can set your mind; there is ample opportunity for alternatives. Often an alternative can be more productive, solve your problems better, help the organization better. You just need a mind opener to open your mind to a more productive, less limiting mind-set. How often do we say 'He could do it if he just put his mind to it'?

The results we get are more dependent on how we set our minds than on how 'good' our minds are in the first place. Consider how powerful a computer any one of our minds is. The neo cortex in our brain is made of 12 to 15 billion nerve cells called 'neurons'. Each neuron is capable of interacting with other neurons in its vicinity. So there are trillions of potential interactions. These interactions form the computer power of any mind. Is it really crucial whether one mind has 13 billion nerve cells and another only 12 billion?

Looked at differently, consider the complexity of running all the telephone networks in every country in the world across all the world. Consider the computer power needed to run all the telephones and all the connections. This power is equivalent to using a human brain the size of a peanut—and all our brains are far bigger than that! Is it really crucial to the results whether one person needs to use up a part of the brain the size of a big peanut to generate this feat while another could get away with a slightly smaller peanut? What *is* crucial is how we 'set' our minds.

As a simple example, if you adopt a mind-set, based on a few instances, that 'Smith is no good as a manager', your brain will be able to find vivid examples to reinforce that viewpoint—including sometimes misinterpreting things in a way that shows Smith in a bad light. You will not be able to see any good in any suggestion made by Smith.

You may benefit from a mind opener that will trigger your brain to consider 'Smith *is* good at several things; how can I get even more from him?'

Another example: adopt a mind-set that 'Headquarters are

too far removed from the business and don't know what they are talking about' and the brain will find all sorts of instances, past and present, to reinforce that mind-set. So suggestions from Headquarters on the business will be disregarded.

You may benefit from a mind opener that will trigger your brain to consider 'These people are not stupid—what good is there in their suggestions?' The brain will then focus on finding the ideas and parts of suggestions that will help you.

Your power and potential are far more constrained by the limited mind-sets you adopt than by how good your mind is in the first place.

The power and potential of your organization are far more constrained by its limiting collective mind-sets than by the collective brain-power within it.

Consider, for example, whether one of the following organizations is more likely to succeed than the other or whether they both have the same potential:

(a) Organization 'A' that is currently getting the right answers to the wrong questions.
(b) Organization 'B' that is currently getting the wrong answers to the right questions.

Short-term, there may be little difference between A and B. But over even the medium-term, organization B will win. The reason is that eventually the power of the minds in the organization will find the right answers. The key is setting the right questions for the brain-power to focus on.

By contrast, organization A will not get to the right questions—its people will be congratulating themselves on how clever they are in getting the right answers to the questions they have set themselves. Their minds will be closed.

Unfortunately, our culture dictates this self-defeating spiral. Teachers ask questions. Pupils give answers. Pupils vie with each other to get the right answer first. 'Hands up, who has the answer.' Pupils are fast to correct another who has got the wrong answer. They will vie with one another to get a better answer and so show how clever they are. Their collective brain-power will eventually get the right answer to the teacher's question.

As with pupils, so with organizations.

What our culture does not encourage is questioning whether we have the right question. The teacher or the boss asks the questions, the pupils or the organization exercise their minds to find the right answer. To question the validity of the question is almost impertinent. So the collective mind-set is rarely questioned.

A practical example

Consider an organization in which the level of profits is too low. The way you set out to change this is the way you achieve any 'bigger and better' thing. The method, as we discussed before, is fairly simple:

- Set new, stretching goals.
- Find better ways to reach them.

If the organization has been improving profits on average by five per cent a year for several years, a 'stretching' question might be:

- 'How can we grow profits 10 per cent or 15 per cent a year?'

Assume, however, that you come in as a 'new broom' at the

top with a different mind-set and ask the question:

• 'How can we *double* profits in two years?'

What happens? Because of the history and mind-sets, this concept will be rejected: 'It simply can't be done'; 'Don't be stupid'; 'It's impractical'; etc.

Moreover, when you address what 'better ways' the organization can find to reach this stretching goal, each will probably be rejected on the grounds that it won't work with the mind-sets as follows:

• 'We cannot reduce the cost of the products, because that will reduce quality, and we'll lose sales and so lose more profit than we will gain.'
• 'We cannot increase the price because that will also lose sales and lose us more profit than we gain.'
• 'We cannot reduce the marketing expense because that will lose us sales and will lose us more than we gain.'
• 'On the other hand, if we increase marketing support, we don't think we can get more sales because the market is flat, so profit will go down because of the extra cost.'
• 'We cannot reduce the cost of our sales force, because that will mean fewer people, fewer calls on customers, fewer sales and so less profit.'
• 'We cannot reduce our overhead cost because that will reduce the amount of projects we can do and put at risk the things that have brought our current five per cent profit success.'

Net, the organization has—unknowingly—limited mind-sets that reject the notion of 'doubling the profits in two years' and reject every new way suggested of achieving it.

On the other hand, there could be very different answers and results if you could find a way of opening up the minds to the *possibility* of achieving the goal and if you could get a collective mind-set that focuses all the intelligence and energy of the organization on *how* it might be done. Then:

- With a new mind-set, the organization may find that products are over-engineered and a change in product— to one of lower cost—might well not be noticeable or important to customers. Indeed, by eliminating cost in some aspects of low importance, it might be possible to fund an improvement in an aspect of higher importance, whilst still reducing overall cost.

    If this concept wasn't applicable to all the products, it might still be applicable to some.
- With a different mind-set, the organization may find that the products are not price-sensitive; that price increases can be taken. If this is not applicable to all the products, it may still be applicable to some products, some sizes or some variants—at least some of the time.
- With a different mind-set, the organization may find that not all of the marketing expense is very effective at driving sales. You could identify the least effective 20 per cent, and take 10 per cent to improve profit and invest 10 per cent to reinforce the marketing activities that *are* driving the business. Then marketing costs would go down and improve profits that way, and sales would go up and so improve profit an additional way.
- With a different mind-set, the organization may find that by eliminating all the sales calls that bring only very small returns for the effort and refocusing some of the time against more calls on higher potential customers, both the costs of the sales force could go down and the volume of sales go up. Again, this improves profit two ways.

- With a different mind-set, the organization may find that sales of some products are not profitable. By eliminating them, profit goes up. Likewise, some variants may be less profitable than others; by eliminating them, customers move to the remaining variants which are profitable.
- With a different mind-set, the organization may find that by reducing overhead costs and concentrating only on the most important projects, the organization may be more effective, not less; by reducing management layers the organization may find it becomes even more effective, at lower cost.

The change here is *not* in the intelligence or skill of individuals or the organization. The change is in the mind-set. Closed minds have been opened to the possibility of achieving a stretching objective. Minds have been focused on how to find a better way rather than on how to defend a restrictive point of view.

Without major changes, the mind-sets of an organization tend to be those that preserve a status quo or bring fairly incremental improvement. 'It has always been like this.' 'Yes, we want to do well and we *are* doing well.' There is often no trigger to make a radical change in mind-set that would bring a *step-change* in performance.

Imagine the power, however, if we could use mind openers to switch ourselves and other individuals from applying our brains in a limited or blinkered way to applying them in a 'mind-opening way' on each situation where we would really gain from a change. Imagine how good it would be if we could do this in our working lives without needing a 'new broom' at the top or moving for a 'fresh start'. Imagine the power of simply opening our minds and changing our mind-sets.

Conclusion

As with teachers and pupils, bosses and organizations, so it is with how we run our own brains: give the brain the wrong prejudice to work on and it can come up with all sorts of good ways to support it. Our mind becomes closed to any other approach.

The problem is that often we don't know this is happening and that gradually we are adopting limiting mind-sets that are restricting our potential.

What we need are 'mind openers'. We sometimes get this experience by chance:

'That was a mind-opening experience.'
'That blew my mind.'
'I never thought it possible; it opened my mind.'

The purpose of this book is to provide those mind openers to release that power. It provides mind openers to overcome each of the limiting mind-sets we get, one for each day of the week:

Monday: 'There's nothing in that idea.'
Tuesday: 'Can't see how that can be done.'
Wednesday: 'There's only one way to look at it.'
Thursday: 'Judgement based on the facts says it won't work.'
Friday: 'It won't work; if you do that, this happens.'
Saturday: 'It won't work when it comes to the details.'
Sunday: 'It's just impossible.'

- Avoid the mind-set: 'I don't get limiting mind-sets.'
- Choose the mind-set: 'Choose the mind-sets that help.'

2

The three secrets of mind opening

The three secrets you need to open people's minds are:

1 Use all three 'mind modes'.
2 Do it in a moment, at the right moment.
3 Be impactful and memorable.

Let's look at these in more detail.

Use all three 'mind modes'

There are three 'modes' of the mind. People learn by:

- being *told* things (saying/hearing)
- being *shown* things (seeing)
- *experiencing* things (doing)

Indeed, this is the strength of tools like management courses: a participant gets a chance to *listen* to some theory, *see* some material, and *do* some exercises. It is the opportunity to learn in all three modes that sets apart a management course from a book, a lecture or an article.

It is the same when we learn as children. Our most remarkable feats are accomplished by the age of seven. By that age, we have learned to walk, learned to read and know 90 per cent of all words regularly used by adults. We will have done it by learning using all three modes: through pictures, through listening and saying, and through doing lots and lots of things, later derisively and wrongly called 'playing'.

The 'mode' is defined by how a person is representing things internally—is it being done in pictures, in words or in deeds?

If a person is representing things internally in pictures and we try to communicate through words, it will not work well, and vice versa. Thus for some people in certain situations:

- 'There's no telling him.'
- 'She just doesn't listen.'
- 'They aren't hearing us.'
- 'How many times do I need to tell you?'

How do we know which mode is working? We know the seeing mode is working when people say:

- 'A picture speaks a thousand words.'
- 'Seeing is believing.'

Similarly, when a mind is focusing not on saying/hearing or seeing, but on doing, people say:

- 'Let me try it and see.'
- 'The proof of the pudding is in the eating.'

In practice individual minds do not just use one mode. They use different mixtures of modes and the same individual uses a different mixture at different times.

So to change—or open—someone's mind, you need to try different modes. It is difficult to get through using words if their mind is working in pictures or through experiencing. The way to communicate with and open a mind is by using the mode it is working in—or, if you don't know which that is, by trying all three modes to find the one that works. This is what mind openers are designed to do: they offer pictures (the seeing mode), stories (the saying/hearing mode) and little exercises (the doing mode). This is what makes them so effective. We do need to use all three modes.

To illustrate the use of different modes, here are typical phrases we all use which illustrate a failure to change someone's mind in the hearing mode or seeing mode and a decision to try the doing mode:

- 'There's just no telling him; he'll have to find out for himself.'
- 'He takes no notice of me showing him what's best; he'll have to find out for himself the hard way.'

Alternatively, we sometimes offer different modes, using the following typical phrases:

- 'Is there anything I can say to make you change your mind?'
- 'Is there anything more I can show you to help you make up your mind?'
- 'Is there anything I can do to change your mind?'

The phraseology illustrates each of the three modes.
People's minds can be 'closed' in any of the three modes, as is illustrated by how we describe closed minds in three different ways:

Visual (seeing)
- 'I just can't see it.'
- 'I have a blind spot on it.'
- 'It's not very clear.'
- 'He can't shed any light on the problem.'
- 'He has a limited point of view.'

- 'He can't see the big picture.'
- 'He has tunnel vision.'
- 'It's crystal clear it won't work.'

Auditory (saying/hearing)
- 'It just sounds wrong.'
- 'He's deaf to the arguments.'
- 'It doesn't ring a bell with me.'
- 'He's turning a deaf ear.'
- 'A voice tells me it's right.'
- 'It's coming through loud and clear.'
- 'He doesn't listen.'

Kinetic (doing/feeling)
- 'It doesn't feel right.'
- 'He can't get to grips with it.'
- 'It doesn't catch on.'
- 'They can't get hold of the idea.'
- 'It doesn't work for me.'
- 'He can't grasp it.'

Find out quickly for yourself how your mind works in each of these modes by doing the following:

(a) *Write down how many days there are in October.* Do it here.

You may know off-hand, but probably 99 per cent of people go into a saying mode in order to get to the right answer. In fact the only way for most people to remember quickly is to recite internally, 'Thirty days has September, April, June and November. All the rest have 31, except February, which has 28 days clear, and 29 each leap year.'

(b) *Write down instructions for the route to drive from your house to your work.* Do it here.

The only way to do this is 'see' in your mind the way you drive. You picture it and then translate that picture into a set of instructions. Your mind works in a seeing mode on this problem.

(c) *Write down how you tie a tie or shoelaces.* Do it here.

The mind only knows these patterns in a 'doing' mode. In fact to develop a set of instructions, you have to do it in your mind first.

The doing mode is very deeply ingrained as a way of remembering how to tie a tie. So deeply, it is very difficult to tie a tie on someone else. Most people cannot do it from the front. They have to go behind the person and repeat the *exact* doing mechanism of tying the tie on oneself.

Similarly, when asked to tie someone else's shoelaces we often do it from the front—and find that the knot we tie is the exact opposite knot (right over left) of the one we tie on our own shoes (left over right).

This 'mind opener' illustrates the three modes in which the mind works. If someone wants to affect the way you think about each of these problems, it will be best to appeal to you in the mode your mind uses on them.

Now let's look at the second secret of mind opening.

Do it in a moment, at the right moment

There is no time like the present in a meeting or a discussion for influencing the way people think and for influencing the outcome or action. But all too often we are left with a feeling of having 'missed the boat':

'If only I had thought of saying that at the time.'
'I wish I had thought of that point then.'
'What I should have said was...'

Often there comes a time when you want to open up someone's attitude, but you don't know how. Sometimes you can think of a particular course that would be helpful or a book or an article. But the suggestion 'you should read the book' is often not helpful because it has no immediate effect. And a comment like, 'What they said on this course was...' is similarly unlikely to work. The contents of traditional courses and traditional books are not usable 'in a moment, at the right moment'.

This is where mind openers come in.

This is why *mottoes, proverbs and slogans* are some of the most popular and effective management tools. They are simple and easy to communicate. Moreover, they are very portable—usable 'in a moment, at the right moment'. They can be used to change mind-sets and alter a particular way of thinking. Here are a few examples:

'I only do what only I can do.'

'The big don't eat the small, the fast eat the slow.'

'Do unto others as you would have done unto yourself.'

'Don't just sit there, *do* something.'

'Efficiency is doing things right; effectiveness is doing the right things.'

'Behold the turtle; he makes progress only when he sticks his neck out.'

'Risk: You cannot discover new oceans unless you have the courage to lose sight of the shore.'

'Success: Accept the challenges so that you may feel the exhilaration of victory.'

Some managers find mottoes and slogans so simple and effective that they even invest in desk-top ornaments with these words written on them or in pictures on office walls, containing framed slogans or mottoes.

However, the limitation with mottoes, proverbs and slogans is that they are all famous *sayings*. The very word 'saying' reveals that—though they are usable 'in a moment, at the right moment'—they only appeal to one particular mind mode, the saying/hearing mode. If we are more in a seeing or doing mode than saying/hearing, someone reciting a famous saying can seem simply patronising and irritating.

Imagine, therefore, the power of having influential 'seeings' and 'doings', as well as 'sayings', that are usable 'in a moment, at the right moment'. This is what mind openers can do—provide a series of 'sayings', 'seeings' and 'doings' to open minds.

Let's now examine the third secret of opening minds.

Be Impactful and Memorable

Consider these examples of ideas and then the examples of the same ideas *in an impactful and memorable form*:

1 'You should not be selfish; put your country first.'

This is a good idea. It is not as good as:

Ask not what your country can do for you,
Ask what you can do for your country.

2 'You are making assumptions about the business and these can make us wrong.'
   This is a valuable idea. It is not as good as writing down the following:

ASS U ME

and saying, 'When you ASSUME, you make an ASS out of U and ME.'

3 Remind a group considering an Australian business that Australia is a very large land mass for its population, with associated distribution problems.
   This is a helpful idea. It is not as good as showing them this picture of Australia superimposed on Europe:

4 A mind-set is when the mind is fixed in a certain way based on a few facts or a previous pattern. Most conjuring tricks rely on a mind-set, with a surprising revelation at the end. Most jokes involve 'setting the mind' with a form of mind opener at the end called a punchline.

This is a good illustration of a mind-set. But it is better when the following are used to illustrate a mind-set:

> *Mary had a little lamb*
> *You've heard this rhyme before*
> *But did you know she passed her plate*
> *And had a little more?*

> *Some mornings I wake up grumpy,*
> *Other mornings I let him sleep.*

At medical check-ups nowadays, your height is measured first and then you are weighed. You are then compared against what is the ideal weight for your height. I often end up not tall enough by four inches.

Headline in newspaper: Astronaut Marries Star.

The mind openers in this manual are designed to be impactful and memorable. *None* of them are long, complicated problems. Such problems are not only *not* usable 'in a moment, at the right moment', but they are also *not* impactful and memorable. Many people will shy away from trying a long complicated problem for fear of being thought foolish when they don't 'get it'. Alternatively, it just seems too much effort—it seems like an exam question or a puzzle for MENSA members. Most people give up trying almost at once and so the effect is lost. People close their minds to the possibility of solving the problem.

By contrast, very short mind openers are both impactful

and memorable, *and* open the mind. This is why 'riddles' are so effective: you can remember both the question and the answer in your head.

We need mind openers that are as short and sharp as riddles, slogans, or proverbs. When you have finished reading this manual, why not go back and choose your favourite 'sayings', 'seeings', or 'doings' to change people's mind-sets 'in a moment, at the right moment'?

Conclusion

To open someone's mind, get them to see things in their mind, say things in their mind and do things in their mind. Make it fast and snappy. And memorable.

3: Monday

'There's nothing in that idea.'

Look for the other half of the picture.

There is a limiting mind-set for each day of the week, and each of the next chapters will give you the mind openers you need to tackle each of them and turn them into a more helpful mind-set.

Monday's limiting mind-set is all too frequent. We reject ideas or suggestions made to us because they are 'clearly' of no use to us. We even have a word for it—it's called *dismissing* an idea. The mind-set that allows us to do this is one of the most frequent and most limiting mind-sets affecting our ability to do bigger and better things.

Many suggestions for improvement are instantly rejected—simply because our initial reaction to them is 'there's nothing in it'. Once we've decided that, our minds can be very, very stubborn in refusing to take on board ideas on how to do better. The same happens when you make suggestions to others. New ways to get things done are rejected because people can't immediately see the sense in them. And if people can't see the sense in something it will never catch on or get done.

But people rarely make stupid suggestions. There is always *something* in it. Adopt a mind-set to find that something before you turn your back on any suggestion. If at first it isn't fully clear what the benefit is, 'look for the other half of the picture'. Here are a few ideas on how to do this.

Mind Opener: **Lines**
Do these lines signify anything? Is there anything in this?

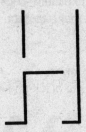

Consider it for a few minutes before moving on to the explanation.

Explanation: It is a block capital letter H, seen from above and slightly from the right, so a few shadows appear on the side of the block.

Mind Opener: **Elba**
This is a picture of the island of Elba. Is there anyone on the island?

Again, consider for a few minutes before moving on to the explanation.

Explanation: If you cannot see anything, you are probably only seeing half of the picture. There is something, once you see the other half of the picture. Look at the figure between the trees. You will see that Napoleon is still on the island of Elba.

Mind Opener: Black and white

Is there anything in these black-and-white images?

Consider this for a few minutes before moving to the explanation.

Explanation: There *is* something in these shapes. It is just necessary to have the mind-set to find the full picture. It is a picture of a left hand, showing the middle three fingers and half of the little finger and thumb, resting on a wall on the right. There is light from the room behind the hand, causing the shades of the fingers to fall on the wall.

Once you see the full picture it's impossible subsequently to look at the shapes without seeing it. But before knowing the answer some of them are difficult to see.

With these exercises you probably *did* adopt the mind-set of 'look for the other half of tbe picture', because of the way the question has been posed. Moreover, once you had found something in the first shape, you encouraged your mind to find something in the later shapes, which in fact are more difficult.

More often than not, people are seeing only an incomplete picture, *without knowing* it, and that's what causes the mind-set of rejection. Consider why misunderstandings happen in an organization. Often it is because one party is seeing only one half of the total picture and the other party is seeing only the other half of the picture. The following mind opener illustrates this.

Mind Opener: Candlesticks

If you were shown the following bottom half of a picture of a candlestick with candles and asked how many candles there were, you would probably conclude there are seven.

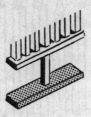

Once you had come to your conclusion, you would be absolutely certain of it and would defend your point of view, criticising severely anyone who thought differently. You might even go further and lose respect for anyone who thought differently, and in future discount their opinion!

However, if another party is seeing the top half of the

picture as shown below, they will be equally as certain that the number is five. Their minds will be 'set' on the number five and they will act confrontationally to anyone who thinks otherwise.

The real situation is shown in the picture below. As so often in the real world, 'reality' is not clear. But, as so often in business, the reason why misunderstandings between the parties are happening is because each is seeing only half the total picture.

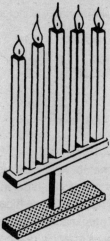

Now apply this thinking to each of the following 12 mind openers. As you do so, see if you can experience the mind-opening moment. Consider also which of these mind openers works best for you. Which are the best two or three that you want to remember and use with others? If you feel you've got the idea after the first six, move on to the conclusion at the end of the chapter. Then come back later to complete the remaining mind openers.

1 Mind Opener: **Water and gun**

A man walks up to a bar and says: 'Can I have a glass of water please?' At this, the barman reaches down under the bar, suddenly pulls out a gun and points it straight at the man's head between his eyes. After a few seconds the man says: 'Thank you very much' and walks out.

What has happened? Pause and think about this for a few minutes.

Explanation: This seems inexplicable. But clearly, if there's any sense to it, you were initially not seeing all the picture. You can find the whole picture if you adopt the mind-set to search for it. The man is obviously quite pleased by the service the barman has given him. So consider what the barman has done. He has put a gun between his eyes and shocked him. Initially the man asked for a glass of water, but the shock he was given met his real need. The 'full picture' is that he had hiccups.

2 Mind Opener: Lift

A man lives on the twentieth floor of a tall block of flats. Every morning he goes down the elevator to work and on returning in the evening he goes up to the fourth floor of the block of flats, gets out and walks up the stairs of the remaining 16 floors. He does not really want the exercise, but he has to do it this way. Why is that?

Explanation: Again, initially part of the picture is missing. You need to adopt the mind-set to 'look for the other half'. If you were told that occasionally the man was able to go up to the twentieth floor on his return and that was when there was somebody else with him in the lift, it might help you get the rest of the picture. Does it? Think about it for a few minutes.

You might also get the full picture if the problem were posed with a little girl in place of the man—a little girl who, every morning she went into the lift, reached up to press the ground-floor button and every evening on her return reached up and could just reach the fourth-floor button. Now does the full picture become clearer?

In this problem, the full picture is that the man is a dwarf and can only reach the fourth-floor button.

3 Mind Opener: Handkerchief

One man bets another that he can lay a handkerchief on the floor and stand on one corner of it, with the other man standing on the other corner, in such a way that the other man cannot touch him at all. The handkerchief is a normal-size handkerchief, no more than 20 inches from corner to corner. How could he win the bet?

Explanation: Again, from the initial picture you put into your mind, you see it as absolutely impossible. You are therefore not putting the complete picture into your mind. The most likely way to stop one man touching the other is to have some sort of barrier between them. This starts bringing up different pictures in your mind, doesn't it?

The solution is to put the handkerchief on the floor under a door and have one corner of the handkerchief on one side of the door and the other corner on the other side.

4 Mind Opener: A 50p soft drink

A boy goes up to the counter in a shop, puts down 50p and asks for a lemonade. He is asked by the shopkeeper whether he wants a diet lemonade or a normal lemonade. A second boy comes in a few minutes later, also goes up to the counter, puts 50p on the counter, asks for a lemonade and is immediately given a normal lemonade. Why is there a difference in the shopkeeper's behaviour? He had plenty of stock of both lemonades!

Explanation: Yet again, the initial picture you put in your mind is incomplete. You need to learn to search for the other half of the picture.

The explanation is that diet lemonade costs 40p and a normal lemonade costs 50p. The first boy put down a 50p piece and could therefore have wanted either lemonade. If he had wanted a diet lemonade he would have expected 10p change. The second boy, by contrast, put down 2 × 20p coins and a 10p coin. He therefore wanted the 50p lemonade, because otherwise he'd have just put down 40p.

5 Mind Opener: Six apples

There were six apples in a basket and six girls. Each girl was to be given one apple, but after they'd all taken one, there was still one apple left in the basket. What had happened?

Explanation: Once again the picture you have put in your mind is an incomplete one. You are probably imagining a basket on the table with one apple in it. Look for the other half of the picture and it becomes clear that one girl has taken the remaining apple and the basket *together*.

6 Mind Opener: Dividing in two

There is a parcel of land, shown below, made up of five squares, which has to be divided equally between two sons. It has to be done with one straight line fence, starting from point A. To what point could you draw the straight line fence and be sure that you had divided the parcel up into two equal portions?

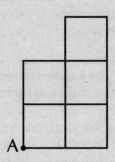

Explanation: This mind opener teaches you *literally* to look for the other half of the picture. If it was just four squares, the answer would be easy: the straight line would be drawn along the diagonal. That now leaves the extra square to be divided in two. If you consider the square as two halves and put one side-by-side as in the figure opposite, it will be clear that the line needs to be drawn to point B. Then the sons will have an equal piece of land.

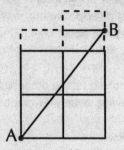

7 Mind Opener: Hot water for a bath

After filling a bath halfway, a woman found that its temperature wasn't quite hot enough, but the hot water from the tap had run out. She therefore set out to heat up some water on the stove in a kettle to pour into the bath to raise its temperature. Some minutes later, her husband walked in and suggested she stop heating the water on the stove because if she heated it any more she'd eventually end up with a colder bath than if she added the water now. What had happened?

Explanation: Once again, your mind probably hasn't initially got the total picture. You are probably seeing a picture of the water still being heated on the stove. In fact, what has happened is that the water on the stove is already boiling. The man points out to the woman that if she carries on just boiling it, then water will evaporate and there will be less hot water in the end to add to the bath to bring the temperature up.

8 Mind Opener: How to Hug

A young boy had never hugged a girl in all his life. He

wanted to learn about hugging and got out a book called *How to Hug*. To his disappointment, when he got at home, he found that it was not about how to hug at all. What had happened?

Explanation: Keep looking for the other half of the picture. He had taken out a volume of an encyclopaedia.

9 Mind Opener: Coffee

A man in a restaurant suddenly realized that there was a fly in the full cup of coffee that he was just about to drink. He asked the waiter to take the cup of coffee away and bring him another one. The waiter returned with a cup of coffee. The man started drinking it—then turned and complained that the waiter had simply brought back the previous cup of coffee without the fly in it. How did the customer know?

Explanation: You are probably still putting an incomplete picture into your mind and that is restricting you. The man was about to drink his cup of coffee, having already put sugar in it, when he noticed the fly. When he added sugar to the cup of coffee the waiter brought back, it was far too sweet. This meant it was already sugared and couldn't have been a fresh cup.

10 Mind Opener: Tape message

A man was found by the police in his study, dead on the floor with a gun by his side. On the desk was a tape recorder. Pushing the play button brought a message: 'I can't go on, I have nothing left to live for,' followed by the sound of a shot. Very quickly the police concluded that he had been murdered. How was this?

Explanation: Keep challenging the picture you put in your head. If the man really had committed suicide after that message, the tape would have carried on running until the end. It would have needed rewinding before the message could be heard. So it was obviously a fake done by somebody else, a murderer.

11 Mind Opener: On the lawn

There were five pieces of coal, a carrot and a scarf lying in a group in the middle of the lawn. A similar group of articles lay on the lawn a few houses up the road. What had happened?

Explanation: Keep looking for the other half of the picture. The children of these houses had each built a snowman and the snow had melted.

12 Mind Opener: Concorde

A man's business trip one day involved him taking the Concorde flight from London to New York. His wife had driven him to the airport first thing in the morning, done some shopping in the airport shops and had waved good-bye to him at the airport terminal. His flight had been on time and had no deviations. Yet when he arrived at New York after his flight, his wife was there to greet him. How had this happened?

Explanation: Once again the picture you put in your mind is incomplete. The man started off his day in New York, where he lived. He took the Concorde flight from New York to London and in the afternoon took the London to New York flight back.

Conclusion

Monday's limited mind-set is a real barrier to achieving bigger and better things. It is the almost immediate rejection of suggestions on how to do better because one can't, at the immediate first sight, see any sense in them. Once the mind has decided this, it digs in and almost refuses to be moved.

Now you have seen this for yourself and experienced mind opening. There are 16 mind openers to open Monday's mind-set and to help direct your mind and others' to the successful mind-set of 'look for the other half of the picture'. Choose from this list those few mind openers that worked particularly well for you and be ready to use them with others, in much the same way as you would use a motto or slogan:

Lines	Six apples
Elba	Dividing in two
Black and white	Hot water for a bath
Candlesticks	How to Hug
Water and gun	Coffee
Lift	Tape message
Handkerchief	On the lawn
A 50p soft drink	Concorde

4

How to use an open mind

Next step: Can-do map

Once you have got rid of a limiting mind-set, what next? How do you use your open mind? Many people think this is difficult. In fact, you can achieve 80 per cent of what you need by using one simple system, regularly. And everyone can do it easily. All you do is draw up a 'can-do map'. The idea of a can-do map is derived from the idea of mind-mapping invented by Tony Buzan. The can-do map is a way to apply all your brain power to the problem of *how* you *can* do something.

How to make a 'can-do map'
- Simply write down in the middle of a piece of paper the problem you want to work on, e.g. 'How to double profits in two years'.
- Then, using this as the hub of a wheel, write the general ideas that come to you of how to do it on spokes coming out of the hub, e.g. one spoke may have pricing on it, another sales, another costs.
- Aim to have sub-spokes off each of the main spokes as sub-sets of ideas come to you. Go on and on with spokes and sub-spokes, filling the page as necessary.
- Use pictures and symbols as much as you can to bring ideas to life.
- Use colours as much as you can; make each item multi-coloured.

- Use arrows to link ideas: use symbols to link ideas.

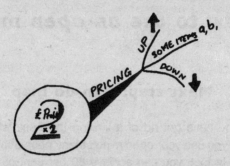

Look for beginnings of ideas and make them better with further spokes. Look for concepts or directions and improve them with further spokes. In a group, each individual can do a can-do map, then explain it to the others, then each can improve on their own. Can-do maps are the way of the future: they can be transmitted by fax, some in colour; they can be copied in colour; they can be done on computer note-pads.

You will find that applying a can-do map to any problem/opportunity you face, once the mind has been opened, will give you more than enough ideas to achieve bigger and better things.

Why do can-do maps work?

There are six reasons why a can-do map works, once the mind has been opened:

1 Although people may say they now have a more open mind, this is often no more than a half-hearted commitment to open-mindedness. They are often more than ready to slip back into their previous closed mind-set as soon as it is acceptable to do so. Drawing up a can-do map is *doing*

something, immediately, to demonstrate the open-mind, and reinforces the open mind. People will be judged by their deeds, not just by their words. A can-do map is an opportunity to *do* something.

2 The can-do map focuses all the power of the mind on *how* things might be done, including how obstacles can be overcome, instead of using that power to cement limiting mind-sets.

3 The can-do map uses all three modes of the mind: you are doing something; you are saying something; you are seeing something (the map and its pictures).

4 The can-do map uses both sides of the brain: the logical left and the creative right. Using colours is a trigger to adding the creative right to the power of the logical left. This is because the right brain controls colour; the left brain works in black and white, like most paperwork, lists and books. By simply using a variety of colours you activate the right brain automatically.

5 The can-do map allows people to draw out ideas in a 'rough' way, to legitimately doodle a little, to generate ideas and thoughts without being exact. It is in line with instructions like 'sketch me out a rough proposal', 'draw me up an outline plan', 'rough out a solution'. All these instructions involve 'picture' words, and a sense of 'giving the idea' without the exactitude of a final document. Because of this freedom, people will actually enjoy making the map. Because they enjoy it, they'll carry on doing it.

By contrast, ask someone to 'write up' a plan, and it is less likely to be done at once. It requires too much effort, it is too final a commitment and we're afraid of being judged on it. It's too difficult to sort out the priorities, too difficult to get the language exactly right, so we shy away from it.

6 Just like a mind opener, the can-do map:
   • uses all three mind modes
   • can be done 'in a moment, at the right moment'
   • is impactful and memorable

Mind openers and can-do maps need to be used with lightness and humour to be effective—no one likes to be told directly that they have a closed mind. But allow someone to 'get the message' gently and you will be amazed at the way their mind will open—in a desperate effort to be thought unbiased and unprejudiced and open-minded!

Let's take another look at our example of doubling profits in two years. This is the 'bigger and better thing' we want to achieve. Let's assume one idea that has been suggested is 'Move the office to London'.

At first sight, to you, this seems stupid. It increases costs and you can't see how it would help double profits. The first instinct is to reject it—and with it reject also the person making the suggestion. On the other hand, it has been suggested by someone sensible and you can now apply Monday's more successful mind-set of 'look for the other half of the picture'.

Set up a can-do map. At the centre put the goal and the idea as shown below. Put three spokes out from the centre to trigger what's *good* about the idea, what's *bad* about it and what's *interesting* about it. Be ready to use 'how-fix' triangles to trigger ways to fix negatives and overcome problems. These are simply junction points at the end of those ideas which are *negative* to the goal: you use them as starting-points for new ideas to eliminate, offset or overcome the negative point. This keeps all thoughts flowing towards the goal of doubling profits in two years.

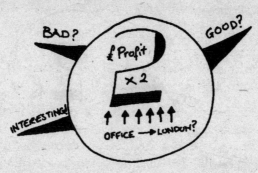

Now let your whole mind focus on ideas. As they occur, note them and add them to your map.

For instance, the 'What's good' branch may trigger thoughts like: *closer* to customers; *more* customers; charge them higher fees or London prices; more availability of the range of qualified staff you need; better location for stimulus of ideas. Each of these can spark other thoughts that may help the goal—for example, 'closer to customers' can lead to: lower travel costs; more repeat business; *which* repeat business do we want?

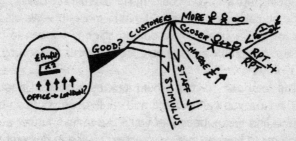

Each can-do branch can be expanded for as long as is helpful.

Now let's look at the 'What's bad' branch with 'how-fix' triangles.

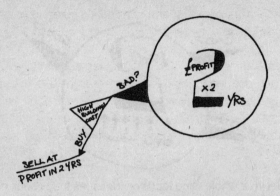

Immediately high building costs and high relocation costs come to mind. Applying 'how-fix' thinking may generate ideas: maybe a building could be bought and then sold at a profit in two years' time—thereby making a direct, real contribution to 'doubling the profits in two years'!

Under the 'What's interesting' branch may be thoughts like 'Why London?' If the cost of London is too high, you might want to keep the idea of moving, but change to a lower cost city; or move to a place where property values are going up and you could make a profit on buying an office by selling in two years' time; or move to a two-office system with a small, single-person office in London to be close to customers and the balance in a lower cost 'country' location.

The total can-do map would look as shown on pages 50–51. Now you can sit back and sift through your can-do map to find those ideas that you'd like to take further and which could help double the profit in two years. Remember that the sub-spokes of the map can also generate ideas. For example, you may decide to take the 'good' idea of seeking repeat business from customers, but change it to identifying exactly who the key customers are and what the likely repeat business is, and considering what other ways there may be to achieve it.

'There's nothing in that idea' is a real progress blocker. But once you use Monday's mind openers to help direct your mind and others' to the successful mind-set of 'look for the other half of the picture', you can use a can-do map to generate the ideas and action that will help achieve bigger and better things.

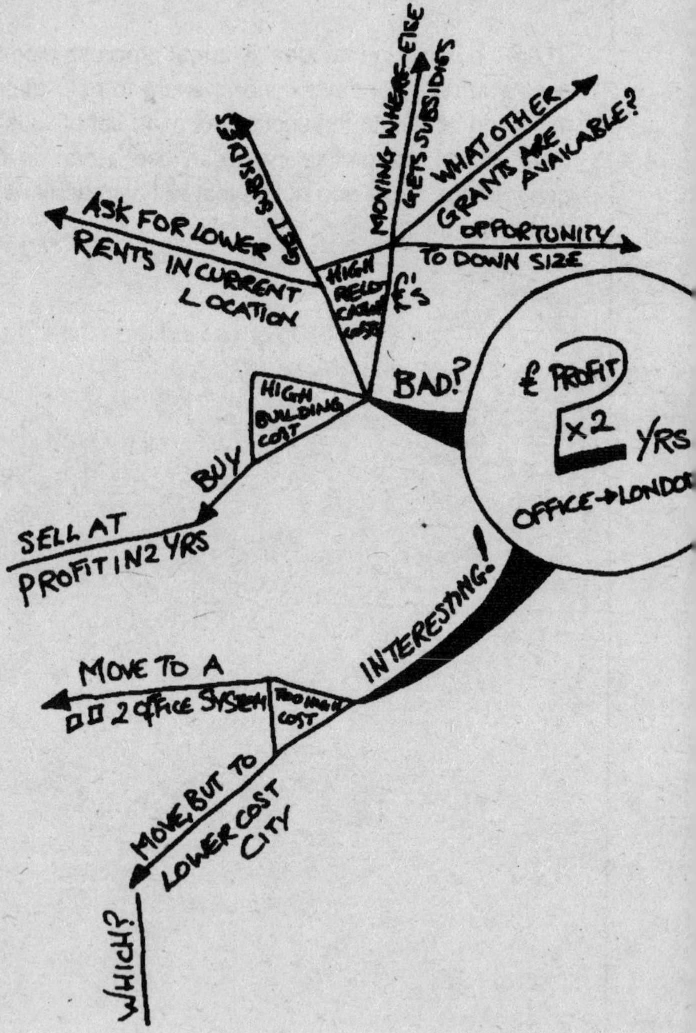
ASK FOR LOWER RENTS IN CURRENT LOCATION
GET SUBSIDIES
MOVING WHERE ELSE GETS SUBSIDIES
WHAT OTHER GRANTS ARE AVAILABLE?
OPPORTUNITY TO DOWN SIZE
HIGH RELOCATION COSTS
£'s
BAD?
£ PROFIT
x2
2 YRS
HIGH BUILDING COST
BUY
SELL AT PROFIT IN 2 YRS
INTERESTING!
MOVE TO A
2 office SYSTEM
TOO HIGH COST
MOVE, BUT TO LOWER COST CITY
WHICH?

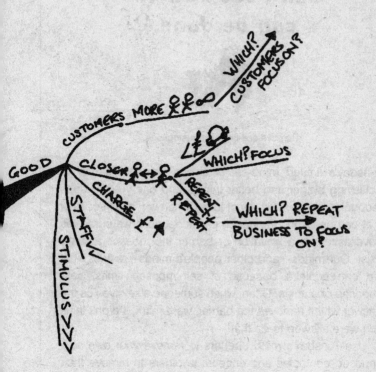

5: Tuesday

'Can't see how that can be done.'

Remove self-imposed restrictions.

Tuesday's limited mind-set is also a powerful barrier to achieving bigger and better things, and one you will soon recognize. We quickly reject ideas when we 'can't see how that can be done'. Very often this is because we ourselves have assumed a limitation or barrier that doesn't actually exist. Our minds—and other people's minds—restrict what we can achieve because of self-imposed limits, self-imposed obstacles. Often, when someone else gives us the answer which removes the barrier, we remark, 'I didn't think you were allowed to do that!'

Use Tuesday's mind openers to remove your own self-imposed obstacles and encourage others to remove their obstacles.

Mind opener: Counters

Consider the following arrangement of counters. Move one counter only to end up with two lines each containing four counters.

It seems impossible. Is it? If it appears to be it is probably because of a restriction you are putting on the solution. Try it for a few minutes.

○   ○   ○   ○

○

○

Explanation: The obstacle you have put in your mind is to think of moving a counter on the surface of the table. You probably have given yourself the obstacle of 'one dimension'. Remove that obstacle by considering that you can pick up one counter and put it on another. Your mind is then opened to an easy solution. Simply pick up the end counter in the row of four and place it on the counter in the corner, making two rows of four.

Mind opener: Rows
You should now be ready for this one. These 16 counters form a square with four on each side. Use the same counters to form a square with five on each side.

○ ○ ○ ○
○ ○ ○ ○
○ ○ ○ ○
○ ○ ○ ○

Explanation: Difficult, but not if your mind has been opened by the first mind opener in this chapter! You will have removed the obstacle that the solution needs to be 'flat' and can consider putting one counter on top of another.

However, don't now restrict yourself with the thought that only one counter per row should be doubled up.

The answer is:

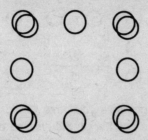

Mind opener: Triangles

Now your mind has been opened this way, you may find it easier to get the answer to the following. There are five matches here, forming two triangles. Use just one more match to form four triangles, each the same size as the two shown here.

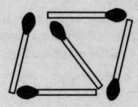

Explanation: You need to remove the same obstacle as in the first mind opener. Don't restrict yourself to just 'thinking flat'. Quickly you will then see the opportunity to 'bring up' two matches, add a third and make a pyramid—which of course has four triangles, all the same size, on its faces.

Mind opener: Cocktail glass

Consider the following picture of an olive inside a cocktail glass made up of four matches. Move just two matches to form a cocktail glass, of the same shape, with the olive outside it.

Can you do it? Again, if you are having trouble it is probably because you are giving yourself a restriction you needn't.

Explanation: You are probably giving yourself the obstacle of thinking the glass has to be the right way up. You may also be adding the restriction of thinking you have to move each match by the whole of its length. Remove these obstacles and the solution becomes easy:

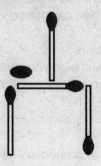

Six 'quickies'

There now follow six 'quickie' mind openers to help illustrate the way your mind often imposes an unnecessary restriction on how you think of the simplest of problems. Be sure to try hard on all six before moving on to the explanations. Take the time to try. Then, as you read the explanations, find the moment your mind becomes open as you realize a restriction has been lifted.

1 Mind opener: Father
A young girl told her grandfather to stop teasing her and 'grow up'. If her grandfather was as old as her father he would be more sensible. How can this be?

2 Mind opener: Tennis
Two men were playing tennis. They played five sets but each won three sets. How can this be?

3 Mind opener: Bus drivers
Two bus drivers are having tea in the canteen at the end of their shift. A young boy walks in and joins them. 'Hello, my favourite son,' says one bus driver. 'You are my favourite son too,' says the other. How can this be?

4 Mind opener: Presidents
The twenty-second and twenty-fourth Presidents of the USA had the same father and the same mother, but were not brothers. How can this be?

5 Mind opener: Sum
The following equation is obviously not right. But how could you move just one match to make it correct?

6 Mind opener: Eleven

The matches below signify the number six. Add just three matches to equal eleven.

Explanations: In each of these quickies you may well have given yourself an unnecessary obstacle in understanding the problem.

1 In the 'father' problem, you may well have assumed that the grandfather is the father of the girl's father. However, a child can have two grandfathers, one on the side of her father and one on the side of her mother. It is quite conceivable, and reasonably frequent, that the grandfather on one side of the family is a lot younger than the other. In this case, the girl's maternal grandfather is around 45 years old, her mother is now 27 and has married a man 20 years her senior. So the girl's father is now 47.

2 In the 'tennis' quickie you may well have given yourself the restriction that the men were playing games against each other. In fact, they were playing doubles together and they won three sets out of five against their opponents.

3 In the 'bus drivers' mind opener, you might have given yourself the horrible restriction that all bus drivers are men. In fact, they aren't. These bus drivers were husband and wife.

4 In the 'Presidents' mind opener you may well have assumed that the twenty-second and twenty-fourth

Presidents of the USA were different people. In fact they were the same man.

5. In the 'sum' quickie, you may well have assumed that the match to be moved was one of the matches making up the Roman numerals. In fact the match to be moved was one of the matches of the equal sign; it has to be moved to make the – into a = as shown below:

6 In the 'eleven' quickie you will probably have given yourself the restriction that the size of the new Roman numeral has to be the same as the size of the initial Roman numeral. In fact it doesn't have to be and the three matches can be added as shown below:

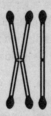

Have you learned your lesson?

Have you managed to learn the mind-set of removing the obstacles you impose on yourself? If so, you could now move to the conclusion and the next step at the end of the chapter. But why not just try a few more and be sure you've 'got the habit' of opening your mind this way?

Mind opener: **Cake cut**

How could you cut a cake into eight equal parts with just three cuts of a knife?

Explanation: This is one more mind opener to remind yourself not to think in your normal dimensions. You cut the cake down the middle in the normal way with one cut. You cut it across the ways at right angles another way with another cut. With your third cut, you cut horizontally through the cake, splitting it into a top and bottom layer, each of which has four pieces, making a total of eight in all.

Mind opener: **Swimming pool**
A man has a swimming pool in his garden situated between four splendid oak trees as shown below:

He is rather disappointed with the size of the pool and wants to double its size, but keep it square. On the other hand, he doesn't want to cut down any of the oak trees. Can it be done?

Explanation: Please do remove your own obstacles. One obstacle you may be giving yourself is that the square has to be in exactly the same orientation as it is now. It could be and should be at an angle as shown below:

Mind opener: Square
Draw a square in which each of the dots below lies on a different side of the square.

Explanation: I'm sure you are learning now about removing the obstacle of thinking things have to be a certain way. Just as in the swimming pool exercise above, this square is on an angle, as shown below:

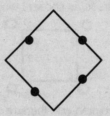

Mind opener: Island

A man cannot swim and needs to get from the shore to the island in the middle of a circular lake as shown below. In the middle of the island there is a tree and there is also a tree at the bank of the lake. The lake is 100 yards across. The man has a rope which is somewhat more than 100 yards in length. How can he best get onto the island?

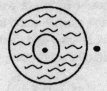

Explanation: The obstacle you may have is of thinking that his first move should somehow be into the water, either carrying the rope or perhaps even trying to throw the rope onto the island. In fact, his first move is to tie the rope to the tree on the shore and then, holding the other end, walk around the outside of the lake around the shore back to where he started from. The rope will wrap itself around the tree in the middle and give him a double rope on which to haul himself from the shore to the island.

Mind opener: One coin

Overleaf is a series of coins where every other coin has 'heads' face upwards (H). The others have 'tails' face upwards (T). How could you, by touching just one coin, make the arrangement into rows that are all heads or all tails?

Explanation: The obstacle you are probably giving yourself is to assume that you pick up one coin and turn it over. But this way of touching one coin it is clearly inadequate. However, if you consider that one coin can push a row, then the

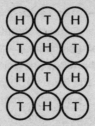

problem becomes easier. Simply take the middle coin of the top row, which is a tail, push it round the table until it is the bottom of the middle column and push the middle column up into the space left by the tail coin.

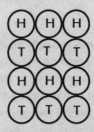

Mind opener: A sum

Using the = sign, one + sign and just the figures 2, 3, 4 and 5, make a valid equation.

Explanation: The obstacle you are probably giving yourself is to assume that the figures have to go together as a number, e.g. 23, or be added together, e.g. 23 + 4 = 5. Clearly this obstacle is not going to allow you to get a proper equation. However, figures can also be used to indicate the square of a number or the cube of a number. The answer is then clear: $3^2 = 4 + 5$.

Quickies to end with

Mind opener: **Sign language**
What are the two most common signs world-wide in sign language?

Explanation: The obstacle you may have given yourself is to assume that sign language is done just with the hands. It isn't. The whole body can be used. The two most common signs are the nod of the head to mean 'yes' and the shake of the head to mean 'no'.

Mind opener: **Hands**
A human being has two hands; apes have four hands. What has three hands?

Explanation: The obstacle here is not so much in the problem as in the solution. The answer is a watch, but we frequently refer to it as having two hands and a second hand rather than referring to 'the three hands of a watch'.

Conclusion
Tuesday's limiting mind-set of saying things can't be done and giving up clearly often gets in the way of achieving bigger and better things, both on a personal level and for an organization. It is often caused by assuming limitations that do not exist.

The positive mind-set to adopt is to 'remove self-imposed restrictions'. An individual or organization that can do this will find all sorts of ways to achieve bigger and better things.

Tuesday has a list of mind openers that you can select from to help open minds this way:

Mind Openers for Managers

Counters	Eleven
Rows	Cake cut
Triangles	Swimming pool
Cocktail glass	Square
Father	Island
Tennis	One coin
Bus drivers	A sum
Presidents	Sign language
Sum	Hands

These should help you avoid the limiting mind-set of saying things 'can't be done' and assuming restrictions that don't exist. You can now move on to how things might be done.

Next step: Can-do map

Let's work again on our general goal of doubling profit in two years. People are giving up because it 'can't be done', since sales in the last quarter have gone *down*, not up; clearly, therefore, doubling profit in two years is just not possible. So use some mind openers to change the mind-set and then start a can-do map. An example is shown on the next page.

In this map four prongs have been put in so far as starting-points to remove the idea that last quarter sales going down means you can't now double profit in two years.

The first prong is 'Sales'. Although the total sales have gone down, are there any products within this that have gone up or done better than others? Have we enough salesmen? Have any particular salesmen done better than others? Are there any new items whose sales are doing

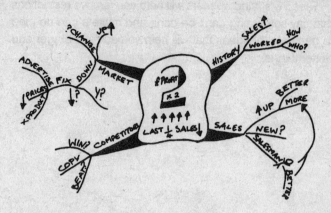

well? Out of this prong comes the idea of focusing more time and effort on items that are doing well, less on others and perhaps putting the better-performing salesmen on the products that seem to have the most potential.

Now look at the 'Competition' prong. Although our sales are going down, are their sales going up? What are they doing to achieve this? Can we copy them? How could we not only copy them but also do what they do even better?

Move to the 'Market' prong. Are our sales going down because the total market is depressed? If so, how can we fix it? Advertise? Change product? If we can't fix the market, should we change all our products, sales efforts and salesmen to working a new market?

Similarly, look at the 'History' prong. How did we get high sales in the past? Can we do it again? What happened last time sales were down? How did we recover? Can we repeat that?

Continue with the can-do map for as long as is helpful. Keep producing the positive ideas. Then sit back, look at the total map and see what ideas you want to take to action on.

Tuesday's mind openers will help you remove restrictions that say something can't be done and make a can-do map to generate the ideas that will help you achieve bigger and better things.

6: Wednesday

'There's only one way to look at it.'

Look at it the other way.

Wednesday's limiting mind-set has enormous power. This is the mind-set that causes people to argue, to fight, even to go to war. Given this power, it is no wonder it can easily get in the way of achieving bigger and better things.

This mind-set has us convinced there is only one way to look at a problem. The way we choose is either the first way we look at it or the way we are preconditioned by our views and experiences.

But there is often more than one way of looking at a problem. The first way you look at something is not always the only or the best way. Adopt the more effective mind-set of 'look at it the other way' and the mind will be released to discover all sorts of other viewpoints and so will offer you more ways to achieve bigger and better things.

Mind Opener: **Men**
What is this a picture of?

Explanation: There are two figures to be seen. One is a very old man seen looking left to right as you look at the picture. The straight line in the middle of the picture is his mouth. The dark areas are a coat pulled up round him.

But there is also a younger man to be seen. His chin is the old man's nose. The old man's mouth is the neck of his T-shirt. He has a dark nose, the old man's eye is his ear and he is turned round from us a little more than the old man, still looking left to right.

Do you see both or just see the one you first saw?

Mind Opener: **One or two people?**
What is this a picture of?

Many people will see it as a person, a man, in left profile. But can it be seen another way?

Ask others whether it can be seen as two people. Most will say not. Then suggest it can be seen as a woman and a baby. Can you see this now? The woman is facing you straight on; she has long blond hair which is formed by the man's nose; her face is where the man's eye is; the gap between his nose and mouth is the short sleeve of her dress; her arm is the line of his chin, holding the baby, whose face is the man's ear.

This mind opener, like the last, shows that things can be seen a different way, once you are shown how.

Mind opener: Man and . . .
What is this a picture of?

Explanation: This depends on how you look at it.

If you tell one group of people it is to do with a costume ball, they will likely see it as a gentleman and a lady, who is wearing a long gown and a bonnet. The thing in the man's left hand is probably some form of handkerchief.

However, if you tell another group of people it is to do with a circus act, they will see the woman as a trained seal, balancing a ball, and the thing in the man's hand as a fish.

This mind opener teaches you that not only is there often another way of looking at things, but how you see things is based on your prejudice or history, indeed on your mindset. Change your mind-set and you can see things differently.

Mind opener: **Double vision**
What is this a picture of?

You will probably say it is a face. Show it to others and see what they think. But first show one person the following sequence of pictures:

and show another person the following sequence of pictures:

Then show them the single picture. The first person will likely call the single picture a lady; the second person will likely call it a man.

Once again, there are different ways to look at things. How your first way of looking is not necessarily the only or best way and may be based on your own history or prejudices. Another way can be equally as valid, or even better.

Instant practice
Stare at each of these figures for 30 seconds or more.

Are there six or seven cubes?

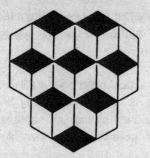

This depends on whether you see the black as the top or bottom of the cubes. Can you see both ways? If not, stare for longer.

Is this coil open on the left or open on the right?

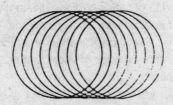

It depends on whether you see, say, the circle on the furthest left being the top or bottom of the coil. Can you see *both* ways? Stare for 30 seconds if you can't.

Is this a box looked at from above or below?

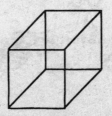

It depends on whether you see the front face as being the one more to the right or the one more to the left. Can you see it both ways?

These 'instant practice' mind openers illustrate simply and vividly that there is often another way to look at things. Adopting the mind-set of 'look at it another way' releases your and others' potential to achieve bigger and better things.

There now follow eight mind openers in which your mind will operate not just in the 'seeing mode', as with the previous pictures. These eight will help the mind operate in a 'doing mode'. We use the term '*look* at it another way' to summarize the idea of tackling things differently. But often it is as much '*do* it another way' or '*say* it another way' as 'look at it another way' – or a combination of all three. Find out how you use the three modes of your mind as you try these eight mind openers.

I Mind opener: Dealing cards

Imagine you are dealing all the cards of the pack equally, one by one, to a group of players. About halfway through your deal, you are interrupted and distracted. You lose your place and don't know where to deal the *next* card. In what simple way can you complete the deal, giving each player the card they would have received *without* counting the cards you've already dealt to any hand and without counting the cards you have left to deal? Stop and consider how to do it.

Explanation: This mind opener gives you practice at 'doing' the problem exactly the opposite way to the way you normally would. Instead of concentrating on where to deal the *next* card, concentrate on where to deal the *last* card, on the bottom of the pack. You know the last card should go to yourself, so deal it; the next on the bottom goes to the player on your right. Carry on dealing, in an anti-clockwise direction off the bottom of the pack until the remainder is dealt out.

2 Mind opener: Sentries north/south

Two sentries were keeping a lookout together both ways on a street. One faced the north; the other faced south. Nothing moved. After a time one sentry told the other to stop smiling. How could he tell the other man was smiling?

Explanation: The first way you thought of this was probably to assume they were standing back-to-back. You probably then thought there was perhaps a show-window and a mirror, or perhaps the sentry could just 'sense' the other smiling. But adopt the mind-set of 'look at it the other way'. The different way of looking at it is to assume they are not back-to-back but face-to-face, one looks north over the other's shoulder and vice versa.

3 *Mind opener:* Dirty face

Two boys were playing on the roof of a shed when it collapsed and they fell through on to a pile of mud and dirt on the floor. One boy ended up with a really dirty face, but it was the one with the clean face who went straight away into the bathroom with the intent to wash his face. Why was this?

Explanation: Look at it 'the other way', through the other boy's eyes. The boy with the clean face saw the other boy with the dirty face, couldn't see his own, but assumed he had a dirty face too. The one with a dirty face could only see the other boy's clean face so wasn't worried.

4 *Mind opener:* More taxi-drivers needed

Imagine there is a shortage of London taxi-drivers. However, currently it takes five years to train each driver, who has to know all the streets and routes of London to be able to find any destination in London from any other point in London. How could you increase the number of effective taxi-drivers immediately? A taxi still needs to be able to go to any destination in London, starting from any other point in London.

Explanation: This is more practice in learning to 'do' things in your mind the opposite way. Simply put taxi-drivers who do *not* know the way around on the street in green-striped cabs. Announce that green-striped cabs are the ones that should be taken by passengers who already know where they are going – they need only the transport service, not the 'finding a destination' service – and they simply tell these taxi-drivers the route as they go.

5 Mind opener: 12:01

You have a digital travelling alarm clock by your bed and are sleeping in after a long-distance flight. The alarm goes off and you switch it off, noticing it reads as follows:

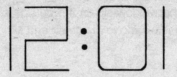

You go back to sleep for an hour or two, at least you believe it is that long, but snap to with a start and the clock reads as follows:

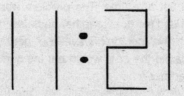

You are sure you haven't slept on for over 11 hours. What has happened?

Explanation: You will hate this exercise at doing things from an opposite point of view.

What have you 'done'? You put the clock down by your bedside carelessly. You put it on your bedside table upside down!

6 *Mind opener:* Seventh-floor window

A man is standing by a full-length window seven floors up in a block of flats. The window is fully open. Suddenly, on an impulse, he jumps straight through the window. He lands safely, on his feet, unhurt. There were no rivers, swimming pools or any other water for him to land in, no trampolines or suchlike to bounce on and he had no parachute or similar device. How did this happen?

Explanation: By now you should be getting the mind-set of doing things the opposite way. The man initially was standing on the window-sill on the outside of the window. He decided not to jump to his death and jumped back into the room.

7 *Mind opener:* Wolf/goat/carrots

A farmer had to get a wolf, a goat and a sack of carrots safely over a river in a boat. But he only had room for one of these in his boat at a time. The problem was he couldn't leave the wolf and the goat together because the wolf would eat the goat. He couldn't leave the goat and carrots together, because the goat would eat the carrots. How did he get them across?

Explanation:
It seems difficult to do. If the farmer takes the goat across first, whichever he brings across next – the wolf or the carrots – will leave him with a problem on the other bank when he goes back for his third journey. However, you are probably 'doing' the trips in your mind, considering taking passengers only one way. Open your mind to taking passengers the other way and the problem is solved. He first takes the goat across. He goes back, picks up the wolf, takes him across, but then takes the goat back with him. Then he takes the carrots across and returns to pick up the goat.

8 Mind opener: Knot
You are asked to hold a corner of a handkerchief in one hand, the opposite corner in the other and make a knot in the handkerchief without letting go of the corners.

Explanation: Please will you learn to 'do' things in your mind the opposite way to your first impression or first inclination? Tie the knot in your hands first. In other words, fold your arms, pick up a corner in each hand and unfold your arms.

Conclusion
Wednesday's limiting mind-set is a major barrier to achieving bigger and better things. If minds are set to look at things only one way, their potential will never be realized.

A key way to achieve bigger and better things is to adopt the mind-set of 'look at things the other way'. All sorts of openings and opportunities will then arise.

There are 15 Wednesday mind openers using 'seeing', 'sayings' and 'doings' to open minds. Choose your favourite from each mode to have several mind openers available to you quickly that will work in each mode.

Men	Sentries north/south
One or two people?	Dirty face
Man and . . .	More taxi-drivers needed
Double vision	12:01
Cubes	Seventh floor window
Coil	Wolf/goat/carrots
Box	Knot
Dealing cards	

Use Wednesday's mind openers to help yourself and others learn the successful mind-set of looking at things a different way. Then use a can-do map to generate the ideas and action to help achieve bigger and better things.

'Judgement, based on the facts, says it won't work.'

Don't let limiting judgement stop you. Question whether facts are facts.

Thursday's limiting mind-set is that facts are facts. You can't deny the facts. So someone's judgement, based on *facts*, is very credible. If a person says that a goal can't be achieved or that there are no better ways to bigger things because of the facts, it is a powerful progress stopper. Once someone's mind is made up, based on the judgement of something as sacred as facts, it will be difficult to open.

However, when such a mind-set is limiting, a more helpful approach is required: 'Don't let limiting judgement stop you. Question whether facts are facts.'

How much of what you 'know' to be facts is based on your personal experience? How much is based on information given to you by others which you have no option but to believe to be true? How much is based on deductions and inferences based on that information given to you? For most people, far less than 10 per cent of what they know is based on personal experience. The other 90 per cent is really open to doubt. So if judgement based on 'facts' is getting in the way, question and re-question the 'facts'.

Secondly, how good is your judgement of facts—or anybody else's—anyway? To attack someone's judgement often seems to be attacking their personal esteem and worth. But no one's judgement is infallible. If judgement is getting in the way of progress, then question it.

First, let's consider the so-called 'facts' we are judging. Here are 10 extremely quick mind openers, using the seeing and saying modes of the mind, that will lead you to question whether facts are really facts.

Facts

1 Mind opener: Sentence

Read the following sentence aloud to yourself and then answer the question at the end of it.

FIVE OF OUR FINEST FACTORY MANAGERS HAVE OFFERED SOME OF THEIR TIME FOR THE DEVELOPMENT OF THE AFFIRMATIVE ACTION PLAN.

How many 'F's are there in the sentence above? What is the fact?

Go back and read it again and check. What number do you come up with? Write the answer here.

Explanation: This is not rocket science. There is absolutely no trick. It is quite straightforward. All you are asked to do is to find out how many 'F's there are in a certain sentence. But only about 10 per cent of people get the right answer. One of the reasons is that in reading aloud, some of the 'F's are pronounced as a 'V' as in 'ov' and the mind discounts these 'F's. Secondly, the mind focuses on the double 'F's and moves ahead towards them.

The *fact* is there are 11 'F's. But not very many people will get it.

If it is so easy to get this fact wrong, how often do you think you get more complicated facts wrong? How often are the facts you are given really correct? If facts are quoted as an obstacle to achieving bigger and better things, question and re-question them.

2 Mind opener: Barrel

Look at the shape below.

How many lines are there in this drawing, do you think? Are there 7, 10 or 15? Give an answer now. Write it here.

Explanation: The fact is there is only one line. Look at it again. Do you see it now?

Once again, if it is so easy to get a fact like this wrong, do you really want to let restrictive mind-sets based on so-called 'facts' get in the way of doing something that will help achieve bigger and better things?

3 Mind opener: Paragraph

Read the following paragraph.

WHEN YOU CAREFULLY READ THE
THE WORDS IN A PARAGRAPH LIKE
LIKE THIS ONE IT IS EASY TO
TO MAKE A MISTAKE. IN
IN FACT YOU MIGHT BE
BE MAKING ONE RIGHT NOW
NOW UNLESS YOU ARE
ARE READING VERY, VERY SLOWLY!

The mind often misses seeing the facts. Unless you read this paragraph very carefully, you will miss the fact that the word at the end of each line is repeated at the beginning of the next.

4 Mind opener: Cylinder

Which of these two cylinders is as wide as it is tall? Is it 1 or 2?

Write the answer here.

Explanation: Again, you are asked here for quite a simple judgement of fact. But, again, only 10 per cent of people get it right. Most people will actually need to get out a ruler and measure the cylinders from top to bottom and across before they will believe that cylinder 1 is the one that is as wide as it is tall, not cylinder 2. Or is that the wrong way round? You will probably want to get out the ruler...

5 Mind opener: Top hat
Is this hat taller than the brim is wide?

Explanation: Again, this is quite a simple judgement of fact, but you will probably find yourself reaching for a ruler just to prove to yourself that it is not taller. It is equally wide as it is tall.

6 Mind opener: Punch bags
Which punch bag is the bigger, 1 or 2?

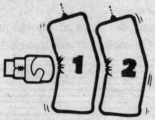

Explanation: Your perception may be that 1 is bigger than 2, but in fact they are the same size.

7 Mind opener: Circles or spiral?
Is the picture below of a spiral?

Explanation: It is difficult to sort this out, but in fact they are separate circles.

8 Mind opener: Arches

Are these arches a continuous shape?

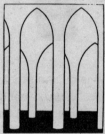

Explanation: The optical illusion can easily lead you to the wrong conclusion. But they are continuous.

9 Mind opener: Line

How many breaks are there in the diagonal line in the picture below? It is another simple question of fact.

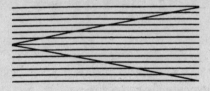

Explanation: There are in fact no breaks in the line, but it is easy to get that impression.

10 Mind opener: Triangle

Is the dot in this triangle closer to the top of the triangle or the base?

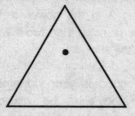

Explanation: The fact is the dot is not closer to the top of the triangle than the base.

So much for being sure about the facts. These mind openers should make it clear to you that if facts get in the way of achieving bigger and better things, question and re-question them.

However, even given the *real* facts of the situation, how good is your judgement of them?

Judgement of facts

Use this mind opener to assess someone's instantaneous judgement.

Mind opener: **Folding paper**
If you were to take a very large sheet of paper that is only $1/10$ mm thick and fold it in half, then half again, then half again and carry on until you had made 50 folds, how thick would the resultant piece of paper be? Would it be 6 inches, 1 ft, 2 ft or more than 5 ft? Write the answer here.

Explanation: It's certainly more than 5 ft. If you were able to accomplish this, which is as close to impossible as it comes, the total thickness of the paper would be enormous. The calculation is 2 to the power of 50, which equals 70,368,681 miles, or more than two-thirds of the distance from the earth to the sun!

So exactly how good is your judgement? Should your judgement, or anybody else's, be allowed to get in the way of progress? Open people's minds to the thought that their judgement is fallible by asking them quickly to answer the following three questions.

Quickies on judgement

1 If a man goes from A to B at 30 km/hr, how fast does he have to travel back from B to A to average 60 km/hr for the total journey from A to B and back again? Write the answer please.

2 A clock takes 2 seconds to strike 2 o'clock. How long will it take to strike 3 o'clock? Write the answer please.

3 The chief of an African tribe wanted to have more boys in the tribe than girls because he needed them as warriors. He therefore issued instructions that each family could carry on having children as long as the children were boys, but as soon as the family had a girl they had to stop having any more children. That way he would end up with families with just one girl, some with a boy and a girl, some with two boys and a girl, some three boys and a girl, some four boys and a girl, etc. He'd end up with an average of more boys. Did it work? Write down the answer, yes or no.

Your initial judgement on each of these three quickies may well have led your mind to the wrong conclusion.

1 In the first quickie, it almost seems obvious that if you travel 30 km/hr from A to B, then you would need to travel back at 90 km/hr from B to A to average 60 km/hr for the total journey. However, the facts don't work out that way. Once you have travelled for half a journey at 30 km/hr, it is actually impossible to average 60 km/hr for the total journey! This is true, no matter how fast you go back from B to A. To understand why your judgement may be wrong, let us assume the distance from A to B was 30 km, so averaging 30 km/hr for the first half of the journey would use up 1 hour. But the total journey is 60 km. To average 60 km/hr for the total journey, means you need to do the total journey in 1 hour; you have used up your 1 hr in just travelling half the distance. You therefore cannot average 60 km/hr for the total journey. It may be against your initial judgement, but it's true.

2 The instinctive judgement for the second quickie is that if it takes 2 seconds to strike 2 o'clock, it must clearly take 3 seconds to strike 3 o'clock. However, think about that a bit more. Two seconds is the time between the first peel of the bell at 2 o'clock and the second peel. When it strikes 3 o'clock you need to allow another 2 seconds for the time between the second peel and the third peel, making 4 seconds in all. Again, it goes against the initial judgment, but it's true.

3 Finally, the African chief's judgement was also wrong. While his logic seems appealing on the surface, it simply doesn't work out in practice. No matter what rules you may impose based on the births that have come before, in any family any subsequent birth has always a 50/50 chance of being a girl or a boy. So the chief will end up with the same number of girls and the same number of boys.

The African chief mind opener is quite pertinent. It says that, in this case, what happens in the future has absolutely nothing to do with what has happened in the past. Whether a family has had a boy or a girl before—or no children before—any subsequent birth has an equal chance of being a boy or a girl. This is a key mind opener for people who reject an idea on the grounds of what has happened in the past. Just because an idea hasn't worked in the past does not mean it won't work now.

If you are still not convinced of the fallibility of judgement, consider these final three mind openers.

Mind opener: Oil and vinegar

There are two bottles filled to the same level, one full of oil, the other full of vinegar. Take a spoonful of oil, put it into the vinegar bottle and stir. Then take a spoonful of the resultant mixture and put it back in the oil bottle. Will there be more oil in the original vinegar bottle or more vinegar in the original oil bottle?

Explanation: Most people consider on judgement that there will be more oil in the vinegar bottle. After all, you have put a spoonful of pure oil into that bottle, whereas you have put a spoonful of only a mixture back into the oil bottle. Judgement says therefore that there is more oil in the vinegar bottle.

But there isn't. There will be as much oil in the vinegar bottle as there will be vinegar in the oil bottle.

Mind opener: Birthdays

How many people would you need to have in a group to have a 50 per cent chance that there would be two people with either the same birthday or a birthday on consecutive days? Is your judgement 50, 100, 150? Write the answer here.

Explanation: Initially, you might come up with quite a high number. Perhaps you might divide the number of days of the year by 2, getting about 180, allow for some overlap, bring it down to 120 and, to get a 50 per cent chance, allow for perhaps 60 or 70 people. In fact, the answer is just 14 people.

This finding goes so much against people's initial judgement that the only way to convince them, short of very complicated mathematics, is to get them to try it and see. Try it on the number of people in your class, training course, management group, shop floor. The initial judgement is just simply wrong.

Incidentally, if you want a 50 per cent chance of finding 2 people with the same birthday in a group, you only need 23.

These facts go so much against the initial judgement that people, especially gamblers, can often make money by betting on this phenomenon.

Mind opener: Julius Caesar's breath
Julius Caesar breathed out air during his lifetime. Air doesn't escape from the planet. Therefore the air you breathe today must contain minute fractions of Julius Caesar's breath.

Is this true? If so, how many molecules of Julius Caesar's breath do you think you inhale with each breath you take? Is the number nearer to no molecules per breath, nearer to one molecule per breath or nearer to 10 molecules per breath?

Explanation: It is true. There are millions times millions of molecules in each breath you take. An average breath actually has 40 million molecules of Julius Caesar's breath! Your judgement is probably so far off, you'd hardly believe it.

Conclusion

Thursday's limiting mind-set frequently gets in the way of new and better ideas. Judgement based on the facts says it won't work. But often facts are really not facts, or certainly not the only facts. And most of our judgements aren't good enough to be the deciding factor in rejecting ways that might otherwise help us achieve bigger and better things. Adopt the mind-set of 'Don't let limiting judgement stop you. Question whether facts are facts.'

Select some of the 17 mind openers in this chapter to open people's minds this way:

Sentence	Triangle
Barrel	Folding paper
Paragraph	A to B
Cylinder	Clock strike
Top hat	African tribe
Punch bags	Oil and vinegar
Circles or spiral?	Birthdays
Arches	Julius Caesar's breath
Line	

Then use can-do maps to generate the sort of ideas that will help achieve bigger and better things.

8: Friday

'It won't work; if you do that, this happens.'

Find patterns that help.

Friday's limiting mind-set is based on patterns. Our minds get set and stuck on patterns they have perceived before. These can really be very limiting. In everyday life, for example, your mind-set may be 'It always rains in Scotland', based on the three visits you have made, during each of which it rained.

When this type of 'pattern' mind-set gets in the way of achieving bigger and better things, it really becomes a problem. It restricts action and prevents things being tried because the mind assumes a bad outcome based on a previous pattern.

In the business example used earlier in this book of trying to double a business' profit, one of the limiting mind-sets was 'you can't raise prices because sales volume will go down'. This was probably based on a previous pattern of it being perceived that sales went down due to a price increase.

To move out of limiting mind-sets based on patterns you need to move to the new mind-set of 'find patterns that help'. Don't accept the patterns that your mind gives you—find more enabling ones.

Thus, given the mind-set 'it always rains in Scotland', seek out the real pattern of weather in the periods outside your three visits. Check whether it wasn't raining anyway in your hometown on the three occasions you visited Scotland.

Given the limiting mind-set 'you can't raise prices because sales volume will go down', seek other patterns that will help. For example:

- Did the sales of each and every product go down on all previous occasions?
- Was there any other factor, such as seasonality or a competitor's action or a shrinking market segment, that caused sales to go down?
- Did sales go down at other periods, when the price *wasn't* raised, and were the factors that caused this present when prices were raised?
- Was the pattern last time that competitors matched the price increase, or did they not, and what pattern would you expect this time?

If you can adopt the mind-set of 'finding other patterns that help', you can open your mind, and the minds of others, to the possibility that other patterns can be equally valid. You can then remove the limitation of a limiting pattern, and open the way to action that brings you bigger and better things.

Practise finding new patterns yourself and with others with the following mind openers. The more you can encourage others to find new, alternative patterns, the more you can release the inhibition of relying on one limiting pattern that restricts your ability to achieve bigger and better things.

Try these seven mind openers to discover how to find patterns, so that you can better find patterns that help.

These patterns involve a mixture of using all three modes in your mind—the seeing mode, the saying mode and the doing mode.

Mind opener: **Shapes**
Two of these shapes have been divided up into four identical smaller shapes. Divide the third shape into five, not four, identical shapes.

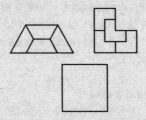

It is probable that the pattern of the first two solutions limits you from achieving the solution to the third. The first two have a pattern of looking very complicated, so complicated that you may almost give up trying on the third shape. The 'seeing' mode indicates it is very complicated.

But in fact it is quite easy.

Indeed, had you given the open square to someone without showing them the first two solutions, they would have found it easier to 'see' the solution. It is quite an easy problem. It is only the mind working on the previous patterns that makes it difficult. We will find that this is often true as we set out to achieve bigger and better things. The pattern of the past can act as a brake, as a limitation. A fresh mind-set can, by contrast, be of far more help.

Of course, there are occasions where a previous pattern *can* help. The trick is to open one's mind to the fact that a pattern can be unhelpful and restricting as well as helpful, and to seek both sorts.

Mind opener: Cutting the cake

(a) *Two people*   You have to share a cake fairly between two hungry children who are likely to argue about who gets the bigger half. How can you do it in a way that both will consider fair?

Explanation: Tell the two people you will ask one of them to cut the cake and the other can have the first choice of which piece to take.

(b) *Any number of people*
Given any group of people, of any number, how can the cake be cut in a way that everyone will consider fair?

Explanation: At first this 'doing' is a very difficult problem indeed. However, it becomes simpler if you build on the pattern you established with two people. Ask the first person to cut out a slice he or she thinks is fair. This slice is then passed round each of the other people in order. At their turn, any one of them can elect to take this slice for themselves. If no one in the group takes the slice, it ends up as the slice of the person who cut it. Then pass the remainder of cake to the next person in the group and repeat the process.

Sometimes it is difficult to see any pattern at all, but once seen, it's easy, as in the following mind opener.

Mind opener: FUNEX
Is there any sensible pattern to this sequence, which was typed out as a conversation?

'F U N E X?'
'S V F X.'
'F U N E M?'
'S V F M.'
'O K V F M N X 4 2!'

Explanation: At first 'sight', it's nonsense. Moreover, to make any sense of it 'looks' as though it requires an Einstein. It is not worth the effort. Of course, these descriptions are using the 'seeing' mode of the mind to find a pattern.

But then try the 'saying' mode. Say the letters out loud. Now it is clearly someone writing down what they heard. 'Have you any eggs?' 'Yes, we have eggs.' 'Have you any ham?' 'Yes, we have ham.' 'OK, we'll have ham and eggs for two!'

Similarly, what is the pattern here?

Mind opener: Sound

Tripe and bananas, stewed *fruit*.
Shave and a haircut, sham*poo*.
Dot de-de dot dot; dot *dot*.

There *is* a pattern here which most British and American people will recognize, though not many other nationalities. Amazingly, however, this pattern has no name, nor any known way of describing it. Try it in your mind in the *saying* mode, with emphasis on the syllables underlined.

You will discover in your mind that each line has the rhythm of a certain pattern of knocking on a door, often used to show it is a friend knocking. It's a 'friendly, slightly fun' knock—'knock-da-da-knock, knock—knock, knock'.

This mind opener is a very powerful illustration of the 'restrictive' power of patterns. A British or American person, given the first half of the knock, would always complete it with the second half. Other nationalities, however, where this particular 'rhythm' is not popular, could answer any number of ways. It is also a good illustration of the need to use mind openers employing all mind modes. In this one, the pattern can be unlocked in the *saying* mode in the mind.

Mind opener: **British**
Here is a pattern almost exclusively British:

Cold Cuts Don't Brown, Can Dry;
Each End Fits Each, Don't Cry;
Dough Can Be Cooked.

What is it? Again, you need the 'saying' mode in the mind to unlock it. It is the rhythm of the national anthem, 'God Save the Queen'. Moreover, if you also use the 'seeing' mode and can read music, you will recognize that the first letters of each word of the rhythm actually spell out the tune of the national anthem:

C C D B, C D;
E E F E, D C;
D C B C.

The mind-set of looking for different patterns in different mind modes can be a good way to open minds from becoming closed on one particular pattern. In the business example used previously, if you can show that sales volume going down coincided with the number of salesmen reducing because of sickness rather than being caused by a price increase, this frees up your mind-set to improve your profitability through pricing. Similarly, sales may have gone down after a price increase because so much volume was sold just before the price increase—as a last offer before the price went up—and, looked at over a longer period, total sales may have increased, not decreased.

'Finding other patterns' therefore can be a real help to achieving bigger and better things by freeing your mind-set from restrictive obstacles. Try these:

Mind opener: **Values**
Letters are assigned the following values. What letter would have a value of 1 if:

A = 2	G = 2
B = 0	H = 4
C = 2	I = 2
D = 0	J = 2
E = 3	K = 4
F = 3	L = 2

What's the pattern?

Explanation: Try the 'seeing' mode': the number refers to the number of 'free ends' there are in the way the letter is written. Thus the letter P would have the value of 1.

Mind opener: **Letters**

(a) Complete the rest of the alphabet:

A   EF HI KLM

 BCD   G   J

(b) Where does the letter 'Z' go in this sequence?

A   CDE HI   MNO   TU

 B   FG JKL   PQRS VWXY

Take the time to try to answer these.

Explanation: These patterns illustrate a key point. If you keep in the 'seeing' mode and keep to the 'pattern' of the previous mind opener, and consider the 'shape' of the letters, then part (a) of this mind opener will be easy. The letters with curves in their shape are on the bottom line; the letters that just have straight lines are on the top line.

However, if you keep to the seeing mode and to this pattern for the part (b) of this mind opener, you will not solve it. You need to change to a 'doing' mode and a new pattern to solve part (b). It has nothing to do with the shape of the letters. Here there is one letter below the line after the first vowel; two after the second, three after the third and so on. The letter 'Z' goes therefore on the bottom line.

Now try these quickies.

Quickies

What are the patterns?

1 A boastful Canadian dog emitted frightening growls, his ivory jaws knifing like mad. 'No one pants quite right,' said Tom, 'unless voiced with xylophones, you zebras.'

2 'J.F. Mam? J.J. as on D!'

3 'I am not even seven,' wailed Stanley, throwing tricycles everywhere.

Try all three mind modes on each. Pause and do it.

Explanations: How far did you have to go into the sentence of each of these before you got it?

1 The first pattern is unlocked in the 'seeing' mode; it is a sentence made up of words starting with the letters of the alphabet, in alphabetic sequence.
2 The second quickie is also unlocked in the 'seeing' mode; it is made of letters designating the months of the year, in sequence.
3 The third pattern also yields to the 'seeing' mode, being a sentence of words of steadily increasing numbers of letters, from the first one-letter word to the final ten-letter word.

Now consider the following group of patterns and how quickly the mind opens up to them:

1 What two letters come next?

O T T F F S S

2 What comes next?

N W R OU IV I

3 What comes next?

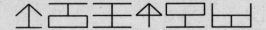

Write the answers here.

Explanations: These may initially be tough. You need the two modes 'saying' and 'seeing'. If your mind is told the *context*, the patterns become clear. The context of all three problems is *numbers*. Now are the three patterns clearer?

1 The first pattern is simply the first letter of the words of the numbers one to six, so the next two letters are 'E' 'N' for eight and nine.
2 The second pattern is the middle letters of the words of the first numbers, so the next letter is 'V', the middle of seven.
3 The third pattern is the numbers 1 to 6 drawn with their mirror image.

Now, not knowing the context, try this one.

Mind opener: What's the next letter in this series?

W T N L I T

Explanation: There just seems to be *no* context to this sequence! Whether you use the 'seeing', 'saying' or 'doing' mode, it seems impossible to find a context in which the series makes sense. So look at the question itself. Now is it clear?

The next letter is 'S' because the letters are the first letters of the words in the question.

Mind opener: Is there any sense in this pattern?

Explanation: Exactly the *point*! There is if you look for it in the 'seeing' and 'doing' modes.

The arrows represent *points* on the compass: SE, then N, then SE, i.e. SENSE.

Conclusion

Wednesday's limiting mind-set often gets in the way of ideas on how to achieve bigger and better things. Based on perceived patterns of the past, we reject suggestions because 'if you do that, this [negative thing] happens'. But often we are trapped by patterns that are not the only possible patterns. To help free up the options for action to bigger and better things, adopt the active mind-set 'find patterns that help'.

Use all three mind modes to seek patterns that help. Use some of the following mind openers to get rid of perceived patterns of the past:

Shapes	Values
Cutting the cake	Letters
FUNEX	Quickies
Sound	Next letter
British	

Then use can-do maps, which help you use all three mind modes, to find the sort of patterns that may help achieve bigger and better things.

9: Saturday

'It won't work when it comes to the details.'

Look at the wood *and* at the trees.

Saturday's mind-set is a difficult one to overcome. Once people have the attitude 'it won't work when it comes to the details', one thing is very likely: that when it comes to the details, it won't work. This is because when people are convinced an idea won't work, they'll tend to work against it and so their prediction comes true. This is a common barrier to be faced when trying to achieve bigger and better things.

The way to change this limiting mind-set is to get people to look not just at the details, but also at the big picture—look at the wood as well as at the trees. If the big picture is right, it is likely that the details can be made to work. If the details are right, it is likely the big picture can make sense.

When limits are put on you achieving bigger and better things, either because people are looking at the trees when they should be looking at the wood or vice versa, use the following mind openers in the 'seeing' mode to help open people's minds to the other approach.

Mind opener: Skull
What is the following a picture of?

Explanation: This mind opener illustrates the difference between 'looking at the wood' and 'looking at the trees'.

Look at the above picture close-up and it is of two children and a dog. Look at it from a distance of more than a few feet and it is a picture of a skull.

This is helpful in understanding the difference between how things look to the 'troops at the front line' and how they look 'back at headquarters'—or the difference between the overview of head office and the detailed picture you get 'on the ground'.

Both views have validity and both perspectives can be helpful. But each party mustn't look at things from a fixed viewpoint. You need to look at the wood *as well as* at the trees. If your fixed way of looking at things is from a close up, near to the problem perspective, open your mind to look at things from further away. And vice versa. Look at the wood as well as at the trees.

However, just looking at either the wood or the trees is often not enough.

Mind opener: **Another skull**

Looking at this picture from afar, it is just another skull. Looking at the details, it is a woman looking at herself in a mirror.

Mind opener: Two ladies

The 'trees' of this picture show two women talking to each other. The 'wood', looked at from afar, reveals it to be a smiling demon.

Frequently, when looking at the details, the big picture doesn't reveal itself. This is the key reason not to be put off achieving bigger and better things just because the details don't look right.

If people's minds can be opened to see that the big picture makes sense, they can accept the details can be worked out.

Use the following to help you see the big picture.

Mind opener: Dots

Do any of these make sense?

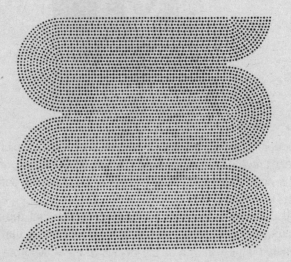

Explanation: Each of these pictures doesn't make much sense when looking just at the individual trees. Look at the wood from a distance and big pictures are revealed: a group of children; and a smiling boy.

The mind openers used so far have employed the 'seeing' mode, because this is the most popular mode for opening this mind-set. There is even the popular 'seeing-mode' phrase 'can't see the wood from the trees'. The principle, however, is as useful when using the mind in a 'doing' or 'saying' mode. In other words, open the mind to 'look' at the big picture and 'look' at the details; 'do' the whole problem and 'do' the small bits of it; 'say' the whole thing and 'say' the parts.

Mind opener: Number in tournament

You are organizing a tennis knockout tournament in which there are 173 entrants. How can you simply calculate the number of matches you will need to arrange, in total, counting every round?

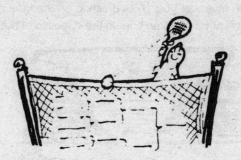

Explanation: This is practice in 'doing' the whole problem from 'doing' the small bits of it. One way to tackle the problem is to work out all the details of the draw, from the byes and the opening round through subsequent rounds to the semi-final and final, and count up all the matches. This is the equivalent of getting the wood by counting up all the trees. The other way is to look at the wood, i.e. to do the whole problem, to get the answer needed. Out of 173 entrants, there will be only 1 winner and therefore 172 losers. Each loser loses in only one match. You will therefore need 172 matches in total, no matter how you arrange it.

Now try the following six mind openers, one after the other, before looking at the solutions. Practise looking at the wood as well as at the trees, doing the whole problem as well as doing the bits, saying the whole thing and saying the parts. Identify in which of the mind openers it is most helpful to take the 'whole' perspective and in which it is more helpful to consider the details, using the different mind modes. Practise using each perspective.

1 *Mind opener:* Two trains and a bird

Two trains start out 80 miles apart and move towards each other at 40 miles an hour. A bird sitting on the front of one train flies off at 50 miles an hour in the direction of the other

train; when it reaches it, it immediately flies back to the first train, which of course has now come closer. It immediately turns round, flies back to the other train and continues like this until the two trains meet. Adding up all these journeys, how far will the bird have travelled by the time the trains meet?

2 *Mind opener:* Lighting up

If you have only one match and you have to go into a

darkened room where there is some wood kindling, an oil lamp and a newspaper, what would you light first?

3 *Mind opener:* Ladder

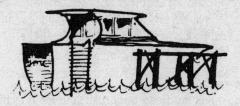

There is a ladder hanging over the side of a boat in a dock. Ten rungs are showing above the waterline. The rungs are 1 ft apart. If the level of the water rises at 6 inches every minute, how many rungs of the ladder would be covered after 10 minutes?

4 *Mind opener:* Tourists

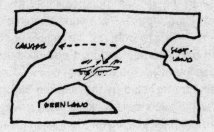

If a planeload of English tourists, flying from Scotland to Canada, crashed in Greenland, where would the survivors be buried?

5 *Mind opener:* Mountain
A man set out at sunrise to walk up a mountain. By sunset he had only reached a shepherd's hut about two-thirds of

the way up the mountain. There he spent the night. The next day at sunrise he started off and completed the journey to the top, arriving at sunset. After spending the night on the top, he found coming down the next day, by the same route, a lot easier than going up and he got all the way to the bottom before sunset. Was there a point on the mountain he passed at *exactly* the same time of day going up as coming down, or not necessarily?

6 *Mind opener:* **Sit on**
What do you sit on, sleep on, brush your teeth with?

Explanations: How much easier would it be to solve the above problems if you knew that in the first mind opener it was best to take the 'overall' perspective, in the second you needed the details, then you needed the 'overall' perspective again, and so on alternately through the mind openers.

1 Looking with the 'details' perspective at the two trains and a bird mind opener, it clearly requires almost a mathematical genius to work out the details of how far the bird flies on each journey and then add up the lengths of each of these journeys. You would need to work out how far the first train had travelled by the time the bird reached it; then how far the second train would have travelled by the time the bird got back to it; then the same on the return, and on and on and on until the two trains met.

On the other hand, it is easier to look with the 'overall' perspective and work out how long the bird is flying for and therefore how much distance it will have travelled. The two trains will meet after one hour, when each has gone 40 miles, since they start off 80 miles apart. In one hour the bird will have flown 50 miles. This then must be the sum of all the smaller journeys it makes.

Clearly, by taking the broader perspective this problem becomes easier.

2 By contrast, in the lighting-up mind opener you really need to 'consider the parts' of the problem, or your mind will be caught out. 'Say' or 'do' the first part in your mind: 'if you have only one match'—clearly the first thing to light is the match.

3 The ladder mind opener requires the mind to go back to *looking* at the big picture. It could get distracted by 'doing' the bits of the problem: at 6 inches per minute water would rise by 60 inches or 5 feet in 10 minutes; the rungs are 1 foot apart so it would probably be 5 rungs. Of course, though, 'seeing' the big picture, the mind will 'see' that the ladder will rise with the boat and the water will never rise to cover the rungs.

4 In the tourist mind opener, the mind can start to wrestle with questions of diplomacy, embassy or airline responsibility, or bereaved family wishes before it 'says the parts' of the problem and realizes that survivors are not buried.

5 An 'overview' helps solve the mountain problem, as does using the 'seeing' or 'doing' mind mode. Assume that instead of one man, there are two. One starts at the bottom of the mountain, one at the top, and they each start at sunrise the same day. It is immediately clear that at *some* point on the first day the man coming down the mountain will cross the man going up it, because it takes the man coming down only one day to get all the way down. When they cross, during the day, they are clearly passing a point

of the mountain at exactly the same time of day. So it is with the same man making the journey on different days.

6 By contrast, looking for a *single* big picture that you can sit on, sleep on and brush your teeth with is to take too much of a global view! Look at the details of the question— it does not ask for a single object that does all three things. The answer is not a wood, but three trees: a chair, a bed and a toothbrush!

Conclusion
Saturday's limiting mind-set of 'it won't work when it comes to the details' can be a real progress-stopper when you are looking for new ideas to achieve bigger and better things. Move yourself and others to a mind-set of 'look at the wood as well as the trees', using some of the mind openers in this chapter. Open the mind to look at both the big picture and the details, doing the whole problem as well as the small bits of it, and 'saying' the whole thing as well as the parts, using some of Saturday's 10 mind openers:

Skull	Lighting up
Another skull	Ladder
Two ladies	Tourists
Dots	Mountain
Number in tournament	Sit on
Two trains and a bird	

10: Sunday

'It's just impossible.'

You don't know what's possible until you try.

The ultimate limiting mind-set is: 'It's just impossible.' Faced with this barrier, the mind just gives up, the body and the organization just stop working. Many of the best ideas for achieving bigger and better things are rejected because someone else considers them impossible.

But does your mind, or anyone else's, really know what can and can't be done? How often are we wrong when we say something can't be done? How often do we find ourselves saying, 'I'd never have thought it possible' or 'That looked impossible'?

This limiting mind-set is the basis, for example, for every conjuring trick, magic trick, card trick or circus act. 'How did he do that, it looks impossible?!' In such a situation, we know in advance that the 'impossible' is going to be achieved—and we are still amazed. If we continue to believe something is impossible even when we *know* we are facing a conjuror or magician who will achieve it, how often do you think we are wrong in everyday life when we believe something to be impossible? Probably we are wrong 90 per cent of the time!

Add to this the fact that what is considered impossible by one generation is often very much possible later on. Indeed, at today's rate of rapid change, what is considered impossible one year can be very possible just a year later. So, taking this concept of progress into account, how often could we be wrong when we say, 'It's just impossible'? Probably 95 per cent of the time!

To achieve bigger and better things it is key to reject the mind-set of 'it's just impossible'. Open minds instead to the mind-set of 'you don't know what's possible until you try'! Then vividly illustrate this with mind openers which show no one does really know what is possible and what isn't, what can be done and what can't be done, until you try. Start off with these seven quickies and see how many you get right.

Seven quickies: What can and can't be done?

1 Find three words that rhyme with 'month'.
2 Find a word that ends in 'mt'.
3 Find a word that rhymes with 'silver'.
4 Supply the missing word:

There are three _____ in the English language: 'to', 'two' and 'too'.

5. Find a word that doesn't rhyme with 'eely', nor with 'elly', but which ends 'ely'.
6 Find a common word (not a Welsh railway station name) which has six consonants in a row.
7 Find a word that has the five vowels in it, in order.

Which of the above do you really think can be done and which can't? It's no good saying, 'I'm sure they all can be done, I just don't have time now to work it out, or to go through a dictionary.' For each of the quickies, take the time to consider it and try to come up with answers, or conclude that it can't be done. Make notes for yourself in the space below.

Explanations:

1 Three words that rhyme with 'month' looks as though it should be possible—and if you spent time and got to one example, it would encourage you to think that if you spent longer, you would get three. In fact, it isn't possible to even find one word.

2 There is a word that ends in 'mt': 'dreamt'.

3 No one has yet found a word that rhymes with 'silver'.

4 It's impossible to find a collective word to describe these words.

5. There is a word: 'rely'.

6 'Catchphrase' will do.

7 'Facetiously' is one.

How often were you right on what is possible or impossible? Perhaps words are not your 'forte', and you feel these are unfair examples. If that is so, here are 10 simple 'doing' mind openers to also illustrate the difficulty of knowing what is possible and impossible.

I Mind opener: **Three pieces of paper**
Take any piece of paper and tear it in two pieces to the same tips as shown below. Holding the paper by the finger and thumb of one hand at point A and of the other hand at point B, pull gently and tear the paper into three pieces.

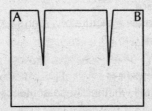

Is it possible?

2 *Mind opener:* Empty bottle
Lift an empty bottle, using just one straw.

3 *Mind opener:* Prediction
Ask someone to write down a three-digit number. Reverse it and take the higher figure away from the lower figure. Consider the resultant three-digit figure; reverse it and add these two together. Is it possible to predict the resulting figure?

4 *Mind opener:* Balance
Balance two forks on a 10p piece on the side of a glass. Is this possible or impossible?

5 *Mind opener:* Tiptoe
Take off heeled shoes if you are wearing them and go to an open door. Put your stomach and nose flush with the edge of the door. Leave one foot firmly planted either side of it. Stand on tiptoe. Is it possible or not?

6 *Mind opener:* Folding
Take a piece of normal paper and fold it in half, then half again. In total, fold it 10 times. Is this possible or impossible?

7 *Mind opener:* Face
Is it possible to draw a picture of a man's face just using the 10 numerals from 0 to 9?

8 *Mind opener:* Sentences
Is it possible to tell whether these sentences are correct or not?

(a) This sentence contanes two misteaks.

(b) This sentence contains three misteaks.

9 Mind opener: Barrel

A man is taking water from a full barrel. He needs to take only half of the water and leave half in the barrel for another man to take later on. He has no measuring device at all. Is it possible to tell when he has taken half the water?

10 Mind opener: A quart

An unfair one for mathematicians only! A cyclist is travelling on a circular track of radius 'n' miles. He goes 't' times round the track. Every mile he travels he drinks 's' pints of water. Is it possible to prove that the total amount he drinks is only one quart of water in all?

Take some time now to try these and decide whether they are possible or impossible. Jot down your answers here.

Explanations:

1 It is simply impossible to tear into 3 pieces.

2 Lifting an empty bottle with a straw is indeed possible. In fact, it is relatively easy. Just bend the straw in two, insert it in the bottle neck, holding one end, and the other end of the straw will flex back and come under the shoulder of the bottle, giving you the purchase to lift it.

3 It is possible. The answer will always be 1089. Take for example the 3 digit number 258. Reverse it (852) and take the higher figure away from the lower figure. Reverse and add:

$$
\begin{array}{r}
852 \\
-258 \\
\hline
594 \\
+495 \\
\hline
1089
\end{array}
$$

4 It is possible. Put the two sets of prongs facing each other as shown, put the coin between the middle of the prongs and balance it on the side of the glass.

5 Impossible.
6 Impossible.
7 The face is possible, once you know how.

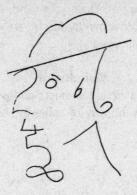

8 It is possible to say sentence (a) is correct. There are indeed two spelling mistakes and there is no mistake in the sense of the sentence.

It is impossible to say whether sentence (b) is correct or not. There are two mistakes in the spelling, but the sense of the sentence is also wrong if there are only two mistakes; but if the sense of the sentence is a mistake, there are indeed three mistakes, so the sentence is correct; but it can't be correct if there are only two mistakes...and so on.

9 Possible. The man simply tips the barrel on its side after he has taken some water until the water threatens to overflow the top edge. If at that point he cannot see any of the bottom of the barrel, he hasn't yet taken half the amount. He goes on taking water until when he tips the barrel the water threatens to overflow the top edge and he can just see the bottom. He will then have taken half and only half.

10 Possible, for mathematicians. The distance the man goes each time round the circuit is 2pi × 'n' miles. He does this 't' times and drinks 's' pints per mile, so his total drink is 2pints, or one quart!

How many did you get? Does your mind really know what's possible or not? Most minds do not, so you do not know what's possible until you try.

Conclusion

The conclusion is simple. Never let Sunday's mind-set of 'it's impossible' get in the way of achieving bigger and better things.

What to do next

Once you have opened a mind and got rid of closed mind-sets, what do you do next? How do you get the positive ideas to achieve bigger and better things?

There are two basic actions to take following this book:

1 Use mind openers to open minds.
2 Use can-do maps to identify ideas on how to achieve bigger and better things.

Both are simple on the surface, but we often find it difficult to take even simple actions. The best way to make progress is to split down these two 'big' actions into some 'easy pieces' to get going as follows.

How to 'get going' using mind openers

1 Memorize the seven limiting mind-sets that get in the way of achieving bigger and better things. Remember there is one for each day of the week. Be prepared to quote them in order, like the seven deadly sins. Memorize also the more helpful mind-sets for achieving bigger and better things, the mind-sets that should take the place of each of the seven limiting ones.

'There's nothing in that idea.'

Look for the other half of the picture.

'Can't see how that can be done.'

Remove self-imposed restrictions.

'There's only one way to look at it.'

Look at it the other way.

'Judgement, based on the facts, says it won't work.'

Don't let limiting judgement stop you. Question whether facts are facts.

'It won't work; if you do that, this happens.'

Find patterns that help.

'It won't work when it comes to the details.'

Look at the wood *and* at the trees.

'It's just impossible.'

You don't know what's possible until you try.

2 Choose your favourite top 10 mind openers from within this book. Make a list of their titles. Then make a list of a back-up 10—so you have even more armoury without repeating yourself. Reviewing this top 20, check whether you have a good mixture of all the three mind modes— requiring the mind to work by saying, seeing and doing. If you are short of any one mode, add some mind openers in that mode.

3 Now 'compose your own' loose-leaf pieces of paper expressing each mind opener, along with the limiting mind-set you are trying to change and the more helpful mind-set you want to achieve. Do these in your own style.

4 Now use these loose-leaf paper mind openers as you would mottoes or slogans. Pin them on your wall or cork-board. Have copies handy. Have them on note paper. Have one format.

Use them at work. Use them at home. Use them with adults. Use them with children. Use them with groups. Use them with individuals. Use them with bosses. Use them with subordinates.

How to 'get going' using can-do maps

These are the way to get ideas to achieve bigger and better things once minds have been opened. They allow you to *do* something with an open mind, at once. They are easy to do. They are *fun* to do. But they can be difficult to do, particularly in a formal atmosphere. There are barriers to their acceptance because can-do maps are unusual, not the norm. To some people they may look silly. To others, with their colours, they may look child-like, like playing. Here are three ways to explain their benefit:

(a) Explain you are using all three modes of your mind, not just one. To illustrate the three mind modes to sceptics, ask them to think of three things and be ready to write down the answers:

- How many days are there in October?
- Give directions for driving from your house to your work.
- Give instructions on how to tie a tie.

Then ask them 'what they were doing in their minds' as they worked out the answers. These illustrate the three modes of saying, seeing and doing within the mind.

A can-do map helps you employ all three modes, rather than just one, as you work to get ideas to achieve bigger and better things. Isn't it better to be using all your mind rather than just a part of it?

(b) Explain you are seeking the accelerated thinking you had early in life. The fastest and best learning of anyone's life is from birth to about the age of seven. This is a time when almost incredible feats are accomplished—learning a language, learning to walk, to read, etc., etc., and it is notable for the obvious use of all three mind modes: 'saying' in terms of rhymes, stories, repetitions, learning a language; 'seeing' in terms of the use of colourful pictures around bedrooms, classrooms and within picture story books; 'doing' as in experimenting with everything, from putting things in the mouth all the way to trying out how to walk.

The can-do map releases the same talents in all three mind modes to help generate a similar accelerated development.

(c) Explain you are working in the way the best minds down

the centuries have developed ideas. Da Vinci, Einstein, Churchill or Kennedy, they didn't type out long scripts or spend time just in one mind mode. They doodled, made short notes, with rough pictures and drawings to stimulate their minds. Are you better off copying the habits of great men or copying the mundane habits of those around you?

Be ready with the three explanations and, once minds are open, start to do can-do maps to help get ideas and action to achieve bigger and better things.

Concluding mind opener

As you take action to use your own mind openers and then use can-do maps, be sure to include these concluding mind openers to illustrate the approach you want.

Mind opener: The story of the two frogs

One night two frogs were playing jumping over a bucket of milk. After a few successful jumps they both made a mistake and fell in. They called for help, but no one could hear them. To survive they had to swim to keep afloat.

After a time they realized that they were not going to be rescued that night—no one would come until morning. Then one frog gave up. He just could not keep going. The other kept saying to himself, 'I *can* do it, *can* do it, *can* do it.' As he said each 'can', he kicked out his legs to keep afloat.

The next day the farmer came and found one dead frog in the bucket and the other, exhausted, but still alive—lying on a mound of butter.

Onwards and upwards

It is possible to go on achieving bigger and better things with the right mind-set, as this simple picture shows.

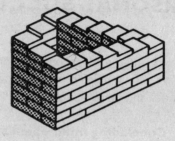

YOUR ONE WEEK WAY TO PERSONAL SUCCESS

Your One Week Way to Personal Success is a simple yet powerful method of creating profound and long-lasting success in every area of your life. It works no matter who you are, what you do or how old you are. And it can be put into practice in just a week.

Find out how to make next week the best week of your life, next month the best month and next year the best year! In one week you will learn techniques for managing your life, yourself and others around you. You will discover what it is you really want to achieve and will have formulated an action plan to get it. And if all you have now is just a vague sense that you want more out of life, here are hundreds of ideas to inspire you.

Give yourself a week to find out what his system can do for you!

YOUR ONE WEEK WAY TO MIND-FITNESS

What is mind-fitness? It is a way of moving ahead by paying attention to the thoughts you feed your mind in the same way you care for the food you feed your body.

Over the last few years many people have started to pay attention to diet and exercise. But looking good doesn't always lead to feeling great. It doesn't make you feel happier in your job or in your relationships. It doesn't stop you sometimes feeling fed-up with life. The thoughts in our minds – and how we deal with them – are what make our lives successful or unsuccessful, happy or unhappy. Our thoughts can limit or liberate us. The most important fitness we need isn't body fitness, it's *mind-fitness*.

So how can we get fit? It's easy! Everyone can do it without much effort. John O'Keeffe shows you how with over 200 exercises and ideas.

Think Good, _Feel_ Good – it's as simple as that! Why not try it out and see for yourself!